A NEW HOPE FOR CHRISTIAN UNITY

Dr John Huxtable, the Executive Officer of the Churches' Unity Commission, was formerly Principal of New College, London, General Secretary of the Congregational Church, Joint Secretary of the United Reformed Church, and Moderator of the Free Church Federal Council. He has been honoured for his work for Christian Unity by a Lambeth Doctorate of Divinity.

In 1972 Dr Huxtable became the first Moderator of the General Assembly of the newly-formed United Reformed Church.

D1741583

JOHN HUXTABLE

A NEW HOPE
FOR CHRISTIAN UNITY

Collins

FOUNT PAPERBACKS

First published in Fount Paperbacks 1977

© John Huxtable 1977

Made and printed in Great Britain by
William Collins Sons & Co Ltd Glasgow

Cover

The Uniting Service of the United Reformed Church
in Westminster Abbey on 5th October 1972,
showing Cardinal Heenan greeting the new Moderator,
the Rev Dr John Huxtable.

CONTENTS

ACKNOWLEDGEMENTS

The author is grateful for permission to quote from the following works:

Documents on Christian Unity 1920-4, ed. G. K. A. Bell, O.U.P., 1924

Outline of a Reunion Scheme for the Church of England and the Evangelical Free Churches of England, Cosmo Lang and A. E. Garvie, S.C.M. Press, 1938

Documents on Christian Unity, Fourth Series 1948-57, ed. G. K. A. Bell, O.U.P., 1958. The Report of the Baptist Union of Great Britain and Ireland on Church Relations in England is acknowledged to the Baptist Union of Great Britain and Ireland, 1952; the Methodist Church's Response to Church Relations in England is acknowledged to the Methodist Publishing House, London, 1952

Vatican Council II, the Conciliar Documents, General Editor Austin Flannery, OP, copyright Costello Publishing Co., Inc., and the Rev. A. Flannery, OP, 1964

Baptists and Unity, the Baptist Union of Great Britain and Ireland, 1967

Growing into Union, Proposals for Forming a United Church in England, C. O. Buchanan, E. L. Mascall, J. I. Packer, the Bishop of Willesden (G. D. Leonard), S.P.C.K., 1970.

PREFACE

RECENTLY it has been in the course of my duty to speak in many places about Christian unity, and in particular about the Ten Propositions put out in 1976 by the Churches' Unity Commission. For the most part, of course, the people who attend such meetings and give me a hearing as the Executive Officer of the Churches' Unity Commission are in favour of Christian unity; but it has become quite plain that some of them have certain misgivings about possible consequences of any move towards unity. Even more, I have been shown that numbers of good Church folk from all traditions find it hard to understand why their leaders make such heavy weather about getting together. Why is there so much concern about the ministry, for example? Does it really matter who ordains ministers, and how? That is but one illustration of the kind of question that has been asked repeatedly. And my experiences when speaking on behalf of the Churches' Unity Commission have often reminded me of the meetings which we had in many parts of the country during the years when we were preparing for the formation of the United Reformed Church five years ago.

The sort of language in which proposals of the Churches' Unity Commission are set out strikes the people I have in mind as heavy and academic. I understand why these documents are prepared in this form; but I welcomed the opportunity to try and say in plainer language what the issues facing the Churches' Unity Commission are. I was also glad to be asked to sum up very briefly the main lessons which we learned while building the United Reformed Church. The risks involved are considerable, but they are worth taking if the people who are most involved can be helped to see clearly what really is at stake.

The Ten Propositions primarily refer to England and its Churches; but they may have some relevance to other parts of the world. In many places British Christianity has carried not only the Gospel but also ecclesiastical division, and still today world-wide Anglicanism, or world-wide Methodism, or the Reformed, or the Baptists, may be expected to take an interest in the British Churches' attempts to heal controversies which have proved infectious. The Roman Catholic Church itself often takes a special interest in the British Isles. New factors in the different countries may well modify considerably what the Ten Propositions envisage; but the old 'issues' so prominent in British religious history are not easily overlooked anywhere. More than one set of proposals for Church union have foundered on the rock of episcopal ordination and the unreadiness of Anglicans to see an acceptable way of reconciling the so-called non-episcopal ministries with those in the historic succession. Perhaps the 'step-by-step' method now put forward by the Churches' Unity Commission for England will open a way for world-wide ecumenical advance. Certainly the Trinidad (1976) meeting of the Anglican Consultative Council looked with a benevolent eye on the Ten Propositions. If it should turn out that our work is useful elsewhere in the world, that would be one more indication of the fact that we are all members of one another and that what happens in one part of the world-wide Church has consequences for others.

This may seem an impertinent hope to those who already have experience of reunion in the Church of South India or elsewhere; the C.S.I. was formed in 1947. We in England have lagged behind in the march towards unity. We need to honour the example of those who have pioneered ahead of us and to be grateful for the influence of those who have served in these Churches and have now returned to this country to share their insight and experience. Nevertheless, we may hope that in such places as are still seeking the way to unity our present efforts may throw some light on the way ahead.

What follows is by no means to be taken as an alternative to the official statements of the Churches' Unity Commission. Rather, it is intended to explain them. I hope that the members of that Commission, whom it is my privilege to serve, will not think that I have through inadvertence misrepresented what they are saying to the Churches. For their sakes, as well as my own, I must make it unmistakably plain that the responsibility for what I have written is mine and mine alone.

JOHN HUXTABLE

Easter 1977

CHAPTER ONE

WHY ALL THE FUSS?

A LOT of people say that they are in favour of Christian unity. But they are part of the Christian minority. Most people are not bothered whether the Churches unite or just fade away. These familiar features of the landscape seem little more than relics of an almost irrelevant past age; nor does it concern them that these ancient monuments serve different versions of the one Gospel.

Some devout believers, however, still hold to the particular doctrines proclaimed by their denomination with great fervour and would tell you that to depart from them in the least degree would spell disaster. Let there be any tampering with the words used to proclaim the message or the form in which the worship is offered and you will be told that you have betrayed some precious heritage which is protected by divine sanction.

Others, and possibly a much larger number, are genuinely puzzled by the disarray in which the Church of God appears. Since there is but one Gospel, ought not those who believe it to belong together and be seen to belong together? It is true that in the course of history various divisions have taken place, so that we are now divided into Catholic and Protestant, and the Protestants fragmented into Methodists, Baptists, Presbyterians, Congregationalists and a good many more. And while it is true that most of the Presbyterians and Congregationalists of England and Wales united in 1972 to become the United Reformed Church, this seems a very small step indeed; important enough to those involved in it, possibly a challenge to those closest to them, but not enough greatly to disturb or change the general position. For a good many purposes these different Christian bodies co-operate, and Christian Aid is no doubt the noblest instance of such working together. From time to time, moreover, these different Church groups worship together. Indeed, the whole Church scene is vastly more cordial than would have been thought possible fifty years ago. What is more, there has been a good deal of talk about Christian unity in the past half century; but as we have seen, it has not come to much, and a great many folk cannot understand why there should be so much fuss, about what seems a simple matter. After all, it is argued, we are all after the same end. What are the obstacles to unity that seem so insuperable? Could it be that the professionals (i.e. theologians, ecclesiastics and lawyers) are playing some dark game to defend vested interests? Or are there real and substantial reasons which most people do not know about or cannot be bothered with, which nevertheless pose not insuperable problems but questions of real importance which ought not to be swept under anyone's carpet?

Any parson knows that the denominational loyalty of most of his flock is precarious. Let them retire from some London job and they will most likely make for the South Coast; but it does *not* follow that they will go to the same sort of church as they had loyally attended hitherto. If they continue to go to church at all, it may well be that they will go to some place not too far from home where they are welcomed and find congenial company. The mobile younger members of the community, whose work now very often demands of them readiness to be up and off at short notice, in so far as they attend church at all are not noticeably bound by loyalty to a particular branch of Christ's Church. They are very likely to go to a quite different one, in their new town or city, either because some friend has invited them, or the vicar called and seemed a good man, or just because this was the most convenient place to send the children. All sorts of reasons can be found, none of them apparently theological at all, or very religious. It looks as if the majority have voted with their feet to declare that 'it is all the same thing in the end'. It is Christianity they are after, not particularly this or that version of it, and if people have been in places like Skelmersdale, where four Christian traditions share one building and worship and work together, they will say that their point has been proved.

Readiness to float from one sort of church to another looks a bit casual and could be attributed to lack of theological insight and deep conviction; but it could be that it arises from an awareness of which the theological wiseacres should take heed. Perhaps they look for worship that is 'alive', for preaching that has some 'relevance' or 'bite', for a community which will welcome them and give them some opportunity of service whether within the Church or beyond its circle. They might say that the reality matters more than the outward form; and it would be hard indeed to dismiss such perception as uninstructed or shallow.

Yet it leaves certain important issues vague and un-settled. It would be very likely that such people would say that what matters is not structural or institutional unity, since all that matters is unity of the spirit. Those who argue in this way often get a good deal of support from at least some Evangelicals. It often happens that Evan-gelicals in Anglican and Baptist Churches, for example, have a deep spiritual and theological kinship without being at all troubled that they are in different communions. The form and organization of the Church is for them of such secondary importance that they can be content with a simple spiritual unity. In England the Keswick Convention is a good but by no means only example of this attitude to ecclesiastical affairs.

Those who hold this view might be shocked to find that they have two different and probably uncongenial allies.

A number of the more radical sort are impatient of Church structures in any case and from their own point of view are understandably uninterested in anything that could be called ecclesiastical joinery. They want a fellow-ship that is freer and more flexible than any they know of at present. They fear that any new institution would still be cramping and rigid.

From more academic quarters comes the criticism that the present ecumenical concern arises mainly, if not consciously, because weak and dying institutions feel the need to prop each other up. They did not bother about being ecumenical in the days of their strength; but what good will it do if two tottering structures merge? Do they really think that this will stop the rot? Surely they can see that this will at best do no more than put off the evil day.

The advocate of Christian Unity has at least this sort of resistance to overcome; and he had better begin by recognizing the force of the points that are made to him. He may well agree that if there is no spiritual unity, institutional unity will be a farce. He can see without being told that many, if not all, of the present Church structures are ill-adapted to modern conditions; indeed, some of their recent reorganization looks much as if the oversight and management people have taken over without anyone asking if their skills are really appropriate to the church scene. He will recognize, too, the force of the point that ecumenical concern has in fact coincided with the numerical decline of the Churches in the West, and he may well ask himself whether, should the days of outward prosperity return, ecumenical fervour would evaporate. Yet he will, surely, know enough to realize that often it is only in times of decline, humiliation and weakness that God can make his people see clearly what has always been true.

It will not do to try to deal with these objections by quoting any particular verse of Scripture; and the advocate of Christian unity will not lean too heavily on our Lord's Prayer for the unity of his followers in John 17, as if all were agreed that this represents the very words which Jesus himself spoke, since that is a point of much argument among biblical scholars. Rather, he will point to one of the quite indisputable facts about the life of the Church in the New Testament times; not because he can draw from it any indisputable evidence about the way in which the Church was then structured. Even if he did know that in those days the Churches in Corinth, Ephesus, Jerusalem or wherever were all organized on the same pattern, he would have to face the very proper question, would that necessarily mean that all Churches everywhere for all time were intended to follow that precise model? He would instead point to a fact which must have astonished those in the ancient world who noticed it: the fact of visible unity.

When the Christians met for worship in those earliest days in the dawn of what was then a working day, the readings, prayers and preaching would be followed by the sharing of the bread and wine, as at the Last Supper in the Upper Room. The congregation might well be what would catch an observer's eye. A small group of a dozen or twenty, 'not many noble and not many mighty'; but a Jew sitting by a Gentile, a slave next to a master, a woman next to a man. All the social barriers that divided that ancient society overcome because in Christ each had been reconciled to God through the power of Christ, and all reconciled to each other. The reconciliation made possible in Christ matches the two great Commandments; love of God and neighbour are indivisible. So the Church is the place where that reconciliation is to be demonstrated; and the message of reconciliation can only be stammered where it is not demonstrated in the texture of the life of the Christian Church. Unity in Christ, made possible by Christ, needs to be visible.

Occasionally, probably at some ecumenical gathering, we get something of the feel of what that would be like; but ordinarily on a Sunday morning Christians go to their accustomed place of worship without a thought that there is some deep disgrace in passing possibly half a dozen churches *en route* (possibly one or two of their own denomination!). We have become so used to disunity that we do not feel at all ashamed of it. In spite of the fact that nowadays Christians of various sorts get on much better together than in former days, we still prefer what we are used to; and all too rarely do we ask whether what we are doing is what the Lord of the Church intends.

If such a question entered our heads, we should probably say that at some point in Church history our fathers took a stand for conscience' sake. This is not the place to review the story of Christian divisions. It is enough to say that it is indeed true that issues have arisen, as at the Reformation or at the Evangelical revival, about which Christians felt so strongly that there was apparently no alternative to separation. Looking back at those critical times in a calm mood, we may think that, as is the way in all such matters, deep matters of conscience were mingled with less worthy human motives and passions; and while we rightly honour those who believed so keenly that they were prepared to suffer and die for their convictions, we are still obliged to ask the radical question whether the resultant divisions really represent the divine intention. There was justification for what happened then, let us readily grant; but if we still live as unreconciled communities, must we not describe our condition as sinful – sinful, the biblical expression used to describe what falls short of God's intended glory? Perhaps we shall not eagerly seek visible unity until we are more ashamed of what we now are.

But what about our institutions? Does visible unity require that all these institutions should merge and develop into one enlarged body, which would have all the temptations to bureaucracy that such a body seems unable to avoid? And would we not be confronted with the properly dreaded terrors of uniformity?

There is a sense in which we cannot foresee the future, and can take only one step at a time. If the Churches covenant to recognize each others' members and ministries that would represent an immense step forward, and as a result unexpected consequences might follow quite soon. But while the Churches' Unity Commission is in a sense proposing to take a step at a time, it is possible to make some provisional response to the question about institutions.

It is quite clear that our present institutions are not well equipped to serve our present circumstances. The economic climate raises the urgent question whether any of them can afford to remain in business indefinitely, without radical change. The fact that local ecumenical projects have proved the best way so far of dealing with the opportunities in developing areas inevitably raises the question whether what is possible in new areas should be impossible in old. The fact that in well over a hundred instances Methodist and United Reformed congregations are working together may well indicate which way the wind is blowing.

That our institutions will have to change, despite their inherent conservatism, seems inevitable; but that there must be institutions of some sort is obvious. Sociological as well as theological considerations point to the same conclusion. If the Christian people in any given country are to support one another and work together in Christ's mission to the world, some organization is necessary. In that sense, the Church is a sociological institution, much as is a trades union or a political party. Isolated, independent units cannot function on a national scale.

More important, Christians belong together in one fellowship, the Church. The whole Church is more important than the local manifestation of it; and logically it is prior to it. For convenience, it is broken down into national, regional units; but these forget their world-wide character at their peril. So there must be some national and international manifestation of the Church as well as the local.

There are those who point to the great historic Churches which trace their origins to the time of the Apostles and can point to an unbroken – or almost unbroken – continuity from the earliest Christian times until now; and they can show how these institutions have adapted themselves to changing conditions. There are others whose histories are shorter. Those took their rise when it was judged necessary to protest so strongly against some abuse or for some neglected principle that separation from the historic body seemed inevitable. Very soon these reforming groups developed their own institutions. Even the most radical and independent of them soon learned the dangers of isolationism and the benefits of interdependence. Nor was this recognition merely worldly wisdom. At a deeper level it reflected the fact that Christ's people belong together. Flock, fellowship and body are words which suggest that community is the essence of the Gospel; and no community can function without an appropriate institution. If there are to be institutions, who are to be their officers and how should they be appointed? So you are at once on to the question of ministerial orders, and all the other questions that necessarily arise when people live as a community.

The question, therefore, is not whether the Christian Church should have an institution or institutions; but what sort of institution should it be? How can it combine unity with variety? How can it be structured so that local regions have as much responsibility as possible without destroying what must be done at the national level? How can these proposed structures be flexible as well as firm, efficient and economic, adapted to mission rather than equipped for self-preservation? Frankly, we do not see that far ahead; but it is some advantage if we can make each other aware of the problems; and if in the new confidence of covenanting together for mutual recognition of members and ministry our ecumenical log-jams can begin to move, there could come the time when we should learn to see how the institutions could be so restructured as to serve the Gospel more truly. Those structures are much loved and to change them requires the sort of determined and charitable zeal which only derives from being more concerned with the Gospel than with the institutions whose only *raison d'être* is to serve Christ.

All the time we face a dilemma. We *have* to talk about institutions; yet all the time we need to bear in mind the much more important fact that the Church is vastly more than an institution. Mysteriously, it is the Body of Christ. There are many who find the institutional life of the Church irksome, boring, and a hindrance to its true existence. That is understandable enough; but for those who share this mood, this question is more urgent than ever: how are these necessary institutions to be so transformed that they are more useful and less frustrating to the true life of the Church?

CHAPTER TWO

WHY THE CHURCHES' UNITY COMMISSION?

THIS is not a history book; but to understand what is now being proposed about Christian Unity some knowledge of the background is necessary. The famous International Missionary Conference held in Edinburgh in 1910 is often said to be the 1066 of the Ecumenical Movement; and of the consequences the tale is often told. It was, of course, a World Conference; and in the intervening years the global nature of the Church and its concerns have become more and more apparent. No inter-Church discussions may neglect the universal consequences of what they do. The World Council of Churches is one reminder of this world-wide brotherhood, and so to a lesser degree are the World Confessional bodies, such as the Anglican Communion, the Baptist World Alliance, the Methodist World Council, and the World Alliance of Reformed Churches. More than that, the Roman Catholic Church is an international organization in a formal degree unknown in any of these non-Roman international bodies; since within them the various provinces or national units may act upon their own authority. No doubt they would consult one another, as Anglicans have about the ordination of women to the priesthood; but some provinces have proceeded to such ordinations, while the rest are not yet ready to do more than declare that there is no theological objection to it. The provinces were free so to act.

In several ways, therefore, the various Churches are reminded of their universal calling and mission. Yet it is important and necessary for them to keep a watchful eye on their duty and opportunity in their own land; and they should understand the ecclesiastical application of St John's observation that if a man does not love the brother he has seen he is not likely to be able to love the God he has not seen. What is the virtue of being in communion with an Anglican in Peru, whom you are most unlikely ever to see, if you are not in communion with the Methodist around the corner whom you can scarcely avoid? To speak about Christian unity with one's eyes on one's own country is not necessarily to be parochial.

Since 1910 a great many discussions about unity have taken place. The resultant statements are increasingly cordial in tone, but their practical outcome is meagre. To read the relevant parts of Bishop George Bell's *Documents on Christian Unity*, for example, shows that the basic difficulties have so far proved insoluble. The Lambeth Conference of 1920 and its *Appeal to All Christian People* evoked a number of responses from the Free Churches. The obstacles then were much the same as we face today: the status of the creeds, the place of the sacraments in the life of the Church, and the ordering of the ministry. There is indeed, as we shall later see, profound agreement about the Christian faith despite the confusion now so widespread and pluralism that is now fashionable. The nature of the sacraments, especially baptism, is much discussed; and it is noticeable that liturgical reforms in the various Churches have resulted, apparently quite spontaneously, in a unanimity of understanding and a similarity of practice which would have seemed a day-dream in 1920. Yet the question of ministerial orders remains.

Turn the question which way you will, you come across exactly the same issues; you are not greatly profited by looking at the issues from a different angle. Archbishop Fisher in his famous Cambridge sermon of 1946 argued that the time was not yet ripe for constitutional reunion but hoped that there could be a process of assimilation, by taking episcopacy into the system of the non-episcopal Churches. No doubt he genuinely hoped that the Church of England and whatever non-episcopal Churches would follow his lead could then enjoy full inter-communion. One cannot tell whether Dr Fisher was surprised or not to find that his suggestion posed almost exactly the same problems as the constitutional reunion to which he had proposed this alternative. Yet those who took part in the resultant Anglican-Methodist attempt at a two-stage reconciliation of the two Churches knew the hard facts.

When, indeed, you realize how often and for how long this discussion has gone on at almost every level of Church life, you can scarcely wonder that eyes become glazed when the topic is raised yet again. What is still more remarkable is that the topic will not die, and that Christians still persist in seeking to make visible to themselves and to the world the unity that they know in Christ. This persistent stamina has no doubt been partly nourished by the example of leaders of vision and courage. From time to time events like the Second Vatican Council have raised and not wholly betrayed great hopes. Christians in various localities have worked together and so come to know and trust one another. One way or another the matter will not rest, nor can we find release from the task.

It is not possible to estimate what has been the influence of the Ecumenical Movement as a whole on the Church in England; but there are two documents of the World Council of Churches which have been so often quoted that they must rank as two of the most important. One came from the Faith and Order Conference at Lund, 1952. 'There are truths about the nature of God and his Church which will remain for ever closed to us unless we act together in obedience to the unity which is already ours. We would . . . earnestly request our Churches to consider whether they are doing all they ought to do to manifest the oneness of the people of God. Should not our Churches ask themselves whether they are showing sufficient eagerness to enter into conversations with other Churches, and whether they should not act together in all matters except those in which deep differences of conviction compel them to act separately? Should they not acknowledge the fact that they often allow themselves to be separated from each other by secular forces and influences instead of witnessing together to the sole Lordship of Christ who gathers His people out of all nations, races and tongues?'

The other which needs noting is the famous New Delhi Statement (1961): 'We believe that the unity which is both God's will and his gift to his Church is being made visible as all in each place who are baptized into Jesus Christ and confess him as Lord and Saviour are brought by the Holy Spirit into one fully committed fellowship, holding the one Apostolic faith, preaching the one Gospel, breaking the one bread, joining in common prayer, and having a corporate life reaching out in witness and service to all, and who at the same time are united with the whole Christian fellowship in all places and all ages in such wise that ministry and members are accepted by all, and that all can act and speak together as occasion requires for the tasks to which God calls his people.'

As far as England is concerned, a convenient point to start this brief background sketch of the way by which we have come is the Faith and Order Conference of 1964, convened by the British Council of Churches at Nottingham University. It was an unofficial conference in the sense that those attending it had not been commissioned by their Churches to attend as negotiators: it was a consultation. Those present found that there was sufficient agreement on the essentials of the Christian faith for there to be no hindrance to unity on that ground. The Conference is chiefly remembered for its call to the British Churches to covenant for unity by Easter 1980. There were those, of course, who thought it wrong to 'time-table' the Holy Spirit; but the great majority felt that to set a definite goal made it more likely that the Spirit would assist us to reach it. At the insistence of Scottish representatives it was agreed, reluctantly by some, that negotiations for union should take place in regions, which was taken to mean that the Scots would look after affairs north of the border and leave the other British nations likewise to deal with the matter within their national bounds.

The text of the relevant resolution ran: 'United in our urgent desire for One Church Renewed for Mission, this Conference invites the member-churches of the British Council of Churches, in appropriate groupings such as nations, to covenant together to work and pray for the inauguration of union by a date agreed among them. We dare to hope that the date should be not later than Easter Day 1980. We believe that we should offer obedience to God in a commitment as decisive as this. Should any church find itself unable to enter into such a Covenant, we hope that it will state the conditions under which it might find it possible to do so.'

At the time this Conference raised high hopes; but before long it ran into difficulties. What would such a Covenant involve? While that was teased out, the enthusiasm waned, but never wholly died. Yet no actual consequence followed, except in Wales, as we shall see later.

After Archbishop Fisher's sermon before Cambridge University in 1946 there followed a prolonged discussion between the Church of England and the Methodist Church. This led to proposals for the reconciliation of the two Churches on the basis of a two-stage scheme. At the first, the two Churches would reach intercommunion; at the second, after a good deal of legal sorting out of such matters as the establishment, the two bodies would organically unite. The scheme was rejected in 1972 (for the second time), because the General Synod of the Church of England failed to vote for it by a sufficient majority, although the Methodists had approved of it by a larger vote than was legally required. For many this seemed the end of the road.

In the same year there was a happier outcome of another negotiation for union. The Congregationalists and Presbyterians voted by sufficient majorities in each case to form the United Reformed Church, the inauguration of which took place in October 1972. All that was involved in the achievement of this union is a sufficiently instructive illustration of what progress towards Christian unity involves to deserve a short chapter on its own.

Very shortly before that union actually took place, though all but the final and almost formal decisions had been taken, there took place in Birmingham a Church Leaders' Conference. Among the many issues discussed by this widely representative gathering was Church unity; and great interest was shown in the formation of the United Reformed Church and a great many hopes were centred upon it. Perhaps this newly formed Church marked a break-through which involved responsibility for some further initiatives.

When the General Assembly of the United Reformed Church took place in May 1973, an invitation was sent to all Christian Churches in England to what came to be called 'Talks about Talks'. Under that somewhat unpromising title, the representatives sent by those Churches discussed whether there was the possibility of a new round of discussions to see if any way of forwarding Christian unity could be found.

Those who attended represented a very wide spectrum indeed. In addition to Anglicans, Methodists, Baptists and United Reformed, there came Roman Catholics and some Orthodox and Lutherans, as well as those from the Congregational Federation, Independent Methodists and the Countess of Huntingdon's Connexion.

It was not perhaps to be wondered at that something like unrelieved gloom prevailed over some of these sessions. Naturally Anglicans and Methodists were not easily persuaded that they could bear 'to go over it all again'. Surely, the verdict of May 1972 would have to stand for a long time, sad as that was. Some of the Anglicans most concerned in the Anglican-Methodist proposals were apparently convinced that a point of no return had been reached; and they were commendably anxious that never again should the General Synod of the Church of England appear in the role of one who has led another up the garden path only to reject the partner at the last moment. At the heart of this anxiety was the feeling that in those proposals the issue of episcopal ordination had been put in a form which, it was thought, was most likely to carry the Church of England : what alternative could now be brought forward?

On the other hand there were those who, perhaps a trifle over-confident because of the formation of the United Reformed Church, felt that there had been a real turn of the tide towards Christian unity. A couple of relatively small logs had shifted, perhaps the whole log-jam would now be able to float downstream at some pace. Others pointed to the local ecumenical projects which in a number of areas appeared to have 'solved' some at least of the problems at a local level. Did that indicate a way forward? Or were we to be content henceforth with a growing number of local ecumenical projects while – no doubt very gradu- ally – the 'established' churches disintegrated? There were those who desired to cut out all the theological and ecclesiastical jargon and urged that it would be easy to unite on a federal basis with 'all who love the Lord Jesus' as the sole criterion of membership. To put that alongside what an Orthodox might be expected to say gives some idea of the range and complexity of the task.

At times, then, the venture seemed doomed; yet some- how something held this group back from saying that the venture was not 'on'. Perhaps the unofficial and much larger conference at Christ Church, Oxford, in January 1974 influenced the course of events. The then Archbishop of York (now of Canterbury) was the spokesman on behalf of those who were confident that a way forward could and should be found; and since very many of the 'Talks about Talks' group were present, they cannot have failed to 'get the message'. So that informal conference, held in some of the coldest weather any could remember, may well have been part of that providence which in the end led those who had been at these talks to report to their Churches that in their belief a new initiative was now possible. They also reported that in their view a new Commission should be set up with a full-time staff so that the responsibility to 'run' the Commission should not be added to that of other considerable responsibilities.

Almost all the Churches who had shared in 'Talks about Talks' agreed with the recommendation. Some of the smaller bodies such as the Independent Methodists and the Countess of Huntingdon's Connexion saw that what was afoot was not in keeping with their understanding of the Church. It was a pity that the Orthodox and the Lutherans were unable to agree to be part of the Commission. What was remarkable was that the Churches who assented to the recommendation from 'Talks about Talks' agreed to finance the proposed Commission for a period of three years – which has since been extended by a further year until December 1978.

The Commission is made up of representatives, officially appointed from the following Churches: the Baptist Union; the Churches of Christ; the Church of England; the Congregational Federation; the Methodist Church; the Moravian Church; the Roman Catholic Church; the United Reformed Church. Consultant observers have been appointed from the British Council of Churches, the Free Church Federal Council and the Board for Mission and Unity of the General Synod of the Church of England. There is also the Executive Officer, the Treasurer and the Field Officer (the Rev. John Nicholson).

How does the Commission do its work? It meets in full session as required, often residentially for twenty-four or thirty-six hours; and usually the agenda for such meetings is provided from the Working Groups which the Commission has set up to consider 'in depth' some aspects of the Commission's work. One such group is responsible for the preparation of material on membership and ministry; another has gathered information from local ecumenical projects and makes contact with such groups as 'ONE for Christian Renewal' and similar bodies which are ecumenical but not formally related to any ecclesiastical structure; another deals with such questions as authority; another with property and man power and all that is involved in sharing agreements and the possibility of a pooling of ecclesiastical resources; and yet another deals with the general question of Church-State relationships. All these working groups are served by members of the Commission, and to some of the groups there are added those whose expertise enables them to contribute wisely to the discussion.

It can easily be imagined that when these working groups report to the Commission as a whole, there is frequently an attempt to do all the work all over again! Nothing is more time-consuming than the revision of documents by those whose convictions are strongly held and who adhere quite tenaciously to forms of words which are more significant in one setting than another. At times the Executive Officer has wondered what order (if any) would emerge from the argument; yet the work done by the Commission in a relatively short time disallows his often craven fears, and shows that out of the clash of ideas real results emerge.

It is often asked why this work was not undertaken by the British Council of Churches. There are three reasons. The Commission deals with England only, whereas the British Council of Churches serves the whole of Great Britain and Ireland; the BCC has never so far dealt directly in Church unity matters; and, when the BCC does not include the Roman Catholic Church, it is good to report that the Churches' Unity Commission does.

The Commission, which was officially appointed by the participating Churches, had three main terms of reference. It was to examine the experience of local ecumenical experiments, and see whether they provided any clue as to the way forward to greater unity; to look at areas where there was little ecumenical initiative and try to stimulate such work in them; and – this chiefly – to see whether there was a way to be commended to the Churches by which they might move closer to each other.

Not unnaturally the second of these objectives has proved the most difficult to attain; but the evidence from local ecumenical projects was instructive. A majority of them said in effect that they did not know how progress should be made, but they were insistent that those 'at the top' should do their utmost to find such a way, because otherwise their work would be increasingly frustrated. Christian education and initiation, common worship, shared buildings and ministries were all exciting and splendid in such a setting; but our present divisions with their varying rites, practices and regulations made such co-operation more difficult than it need be, even when normal rites had been 'adjusted' as far as possible. The task of the Commission seemed to them very urgent. A smaller group took a more isolationist line. They had come to some comfortable local arrangement, with which they were so happy that they desired no interference from 'outside'.

Throughout its work the Commission has kept in close touch with these local ecumenical projects, and in addressing itself to its major task it has kept their needs especially in mind. Initially, the Commission considered the term 'visible unity'. All the Churches involved in the Churches' Unity Commission had said in more than one context that they accept this as an ideal towards which they should work. Some members of the Commission would have preferred to speak about *organic* unity; but many said that this was more than their constituencies had so far accepted. Indeed, for them this looked too much like begging a whole lot of questions.

How should you understand visible unity? Very soon the Commission pin-pointed four essential needs: to share in one faith; to acknowledge one mutually recognized membership; to acknowledge one ministry; and to be ready to share one anothers' worldly goods. This formed the basis of an initial report to the participating Churches.

Before long this 'quadrilateral' was expanded into a decalogue, and the following Ten Propositions were published in January 1976:

1. We reaffirm our belief that the visible unity in life and mission of all Christ's people is the will of God.
2. We therefore declare our willingness to join in a

Covenant actively to seek that visible unity.

3. We believe that this search requires action both locally and nationally.

4. We agree to recognize, as from an accepted date, the communicant members in good standing of the other Covenanting Churches as true members of the Body of Christ and welcome them to Holy Communion without condition.

5. We agree that, as from an accepted date, initiation in the Covenanting Churches shall be by mutually acceptable rites.

6. We agree to recognize, as from an accepted date, the ordained ministries of the other Covenanting Churches, as true ministries of word and sacraments in the Holy Catholic Church, and we agree that all subsequent ordinations to the ministries of the Covenanting Churches shall be according to a Common Ordinal which will properly incorporate the episcopal, presbyteral and lay roles in ordination.

7. We agree within the fellowship of the Covenanting Churches to respect the rights of conscience, and to continue to accord to all our members, such freedom of thought and action as is consistent with the visible unity of the Church.

8. We agree to continue to give every possible encouragement to local ecumenical projects and to develop methods of decision-making in common.

9. We agree to explore such further steps as will be necessary to make more clearly visible the unity of all Christ's people.

10. We agree to remain in close fellowship and consultation with all the Churches represented on the Churches' Unity Commission.

(NB. 'An accepted date' refers to a time agreed by those who accept the Covenant, to implement consequent actions.)

Not every member of the Commission would personally

commit himself to all these propositions or to the 'small print' that accompanied them; but all were agreed that these were the questions that should be put to the Churches to discover how much support for them there existed. The Churches were asked to give the Commission provisional responses to these propositions during 1976 and it was hoped that definitive responses could be provided by 1977. It soon became clear that this was too tight a time-table, and consequently the life of the Commission was extended to December 1978, though a definite undertaking was given that the Churches would not be asked to make provision for its support beyond that date. One way or another, 1978 must be the year of decision.

CHAPTER THREE

A CASE OF REUNION

ON 5 October 1972 a large number of people gathered in Westminster who rarely come to London, together with a good many who know it only too well. The bright sunshine seemed to match the mood of those who were gathering to take part in the inauguration of a new Church. Congregationalists and Presbyterians from all over England and Wales wanted to share in the final act of a drama in which they had participated for the best part of ten years. General Assemblies of each of the two Churches had met in May and had adjourned to meet together on this day to take the final decisions and to celebrate the inauguration.

The morning session in the Central Hall, Westminster, was largely concerned with formal acts, some of which were required by law; but by no means all was formality. The new Moderator of Assembly had to be elected; and among his first duties was that of welcoming the distinguished visitors from all over the British Isles and far beyond. Their spokesmen at this session were the Archbishop of Canterbury (Michael Ramsey) as President of the British Council of Churches, and Dr William P. Thompson, President of the World Alliance of Reformed Churches. One of the many happy features of this morning's session was that an 'overture' from the Churches of Christ to initiate a joint committee between that body and the United Reformed Church was received and warmly welcomed. The Churches of Christ had appointed observers to the joint committee which had prepared the way for the United Reformed Church; and had played a significant part in its work. It was no surprise that this 'overture' was brought; but that did not diminish the satisfaction it gave to those who were delighted that their intention to further unity had been taken up. The eventual outcome of this

new joint committee would, if successful, bridge the divide
between those who do, and those who do not, baptize
infants.

In the afternoon as many as could crowded into Westminster Abbey for a service of thanksgiving; the overflow
were welcomed to watch on television in St Margaret's,
Westminster. The gracious generosity of the Dean and
Chapter of Westminster and of the Rector of St Margaret's
symbolized the rejoicing of many Christians who were not
directly associated with the two Churches now united.

The form of the service followed as nearly as the
occasion allowed, the reformed tradition of worship (in
which, it must be admitted, fanfares of trumpets are not
normal!), but perhaps the most memorable moment in
that service came towards the end when the Archbishop
of Canterbury, the Cardinal Archbishop of Westminster
(John Heenan), and the then Moderator of the Free
Church Federal Council (Irvonwy Morgan) each greeted
the Moderator of the General Assembly of the United
Reformed Church and made a pledge, which is worth
recording, for it could be argued that the promises made
that day were in fact the first steps towards the then
unthought-of Churches' Unity Commission. Each of these
representative figures, addressing the Moderator and the
congregation, said: 'I give thanks with you for this union,
and share your resolve to seek that wider unity which is
Christ's will.' Thus on behalf of the three great traditions
of Christianity in this country there was an initial and
representative response to the new Church's avowed intention, explicitly written into its basic documents, to 'take,
wherever possible, and with all speed, further steps towards
the unity of all God's people'.

No doubt those who were in the Abbey and those who
watched the service on television each had their memories
of the unfolding drama which had led to that moment.
They would remember the discussions which had sometimes
led to more heat than light in meetings of presbyteries and
church meetings, the doubts whether 'it' would ever happen

at all, and finally the sense that the struggle, the pain and the apparently inevitable separation in some cases had been worth it after all.

Not all those who had shared in this prolonged ordeal realized how far back it had begun. In the seventeenth century Presbyterians and Independents had formed two of the principal groups which came into being as the consequences of the Protestant Reformation worked themselves out. By 1662 it was clear that both groups would be excluded from the national Church, because the Act of Uniformity, which all ministers were required to sign by 24th August of that year, was unacceptable to them on conscientious grounds. Some at least of those in these two groups might well have been content with some national Church which had a different understanding of its relation to the state; after all the Independents had not been altogether against state religious appointments under Oliver Cromwell. But there were more theological and religious issues at stake. The Independents in particular were opposed to a fixed liturgy as distinct from a directory, which laid down the form of the service but left the detailed conduct of the worship to the minister; and both Independents and Presbyterians objected to the requirement of episcopal ordination. The differences between the two bodies were real and sometimes acute, partly political, partly theological. Nevertheless, it was often felt that, notwithstanding these real differences, they had more in common than their differences might at first sight suggest.

It was, therefore, as early as 1689, the so-called 'Happy Union', that the first attempt at union between these two bodies was made; but its success was short-lived. In the eighteenth century the differences between the two were increased, because a great many Presbyterian Churches became Unitarian in their faith. Although the Independents – or Congregationalists as they were increasingly called – were open to the same theological influences, they remained substantially more orthodox. Relatively few of the original Presbyterian Churches remained orthodox, and it was not until the nineteenth century, with an influx of Scottish people to various parts of England, that Presbyterianism became again an influential denominational force in this land. Although it never attained numerical parity with the other main Free Churches, its influence was out of all proportion to its size, largely due to the theological leadership which gathered, after a period in London, at Westminster College, Cambridge. The ministers trained there often came to hold positions of considerable influence in English church life.

Two attempts were made to unite these two now rather different bodies in the twentieth century. In 1935 and in 1945 initiatives were taken. The latter had more support, and in 1947 there was presented to both bodies a plan of union which had found insufficient support; but in 1951 the two bodies covenanted together to work together at all levels so far as this proved possible. By 1962 this covenant had been sufficiently implemented for it to be reported that unless further steps for union were initiated a frustrated aggravation would grow in intensity. Accordingly in 1963 the Assemblies of the two Churches appointed a Joint Committee to prepare a Scheme of Union.

What were the main problems which it had to grapple with? After all some of the problems which have to be confronted when dealing with other Christian Churches did not arise. Both Churches ordained women to the ministry and held that all offices in the Church were open to men and women alike. The theological outlook of the ministers in each were broadly speaking similar. The main issue in fact was church order. Whereas the Presbyterians thought of each national Church finding its final authority under Christ in a general assembly, composed of ministers and elders drawn from each congregation and presbytery, Congregationalists, following their Independent forefathers, thought of each local church as capable of ordering its own affairs under divine guidance. While for all manner of purposes such local congregations might combine together for all sorts of religious purposes at the county or national level, it was always said, and truly, that no 'outside' body had any authority over these local churches. Advice could be given and often it was taken and followed, but advice it was, and no more.

The differences between these two bodies could be made to look greater than in fact they were. Whatever the theory might be, Congregationalists had come to recognize that interdependence was at least as important to their common life – and just as Christian as independence, as was evidenced by the formation of the Congregational Church (as distinct from Union) in 1966; and at the same time it was clear that in Presbyterianism there was entrusted to each presbytery and local congregation a large measure of responsibility.

On the level of church order two issues in the main proved difficult. In Congregationalism the final authority rested in the local church meeting; in Presbyterianism the local congregation was governed by the Kirk Session i.e. the local elders. How could these be reconciled? For the past half century Congregationalists had had the services of Provincial Moderators, i.e. ministers in pastoral charge of each of the nine areas into which the Church was divided : but weren't they suspiciously like bishops? Some Presbyterians thought that they could see the cloven hoof!

A large number of administrative and legal matters needed much attention, not least the preparation of a bill to deal with trust and property matters; but a major task was to expound the issue of union to the people in the local churches and congregations. The joint committee issued several reports of its work which were presented to each of the Assemblies and remitted for study to the people. At each stage the joint committee sought to make clear its conviction that it was not engaged on an enterprise in ecclesiastical carpentry, but rather in the light of the history of each Church to prepare for the formation of a Church that would at one and the same time be Catholic and Reformed. No doubt the frequent issue of these documents

and the discussion roused by them at every level of church
life was a large factor in the successful outcome of the
undertaking.

The story of the almost ten years which were involved
in advocating and in the end achieving this union is in
some ways an interesting comment on ecclesiastical psy-
chology. There were, of course, those in both Churches
who felt that birthrights were being sold right and left.
Others thought that to unite with only one other Christian
body was too small an objective, and could only be
persuaded to stay the course on the ground that, provided
that Anglican-Methodist negotiations were successful,
negotiations with the resultant 'body' would be a possibility.
Yet others could truthfully claim that they had never seen
a live Presbyterian or Congregationalist, the one disability
was lamentably possible in Cornwall, the other less possible
but not unlikely in some parts of Northumberland. Still
others – such is the perversity of even redeemed human
nature – would prefer to unite with another body, perhaps
the Methodists or the Baptists – almost anything not on the
actual agenda! It was remarkable, too, how many myths
had to be corrected; confident assertions about 'the others'
which simply were not true; and horror stories which had
to be heard to be believed and usually proved to be without
foundation.

There were those who out of deep conviction could not
be persuaded that organic unity was the will of God or
the 'destruction' of either Church a consummation to be
countenanced. For them Congregationalism or Presbyterianism should be preserved at all costs, undiluted and
pure. Some were of a liberal tradition of theology and
feared that they would be forced into an orthodox strait-
jacket; others of a more conservative disposition feared
that they would be led into some 'liberal' wilderness where
the familiar watchwords were either unknown or, still
worse, despised. In the end it was found impossible to
accommodate those convictions in any scheme that could
be generally accepted; and one of the sorrows of the long-

drawn-out discussion was that some declined to enter the Union. It cannot be denied that harsh words were spoken and sometimes the less pleasant features of human nature manifest; but in general there was respect of the convictions of the minority, as it turned out to be. Certainly, the right to express their views was never denied; and it is to be hoped that with the passage of the years any remaining rancour will be assuaged. What became the United Reformed Church Act of 1972 ensured that such property rights as the non-uniting Churches could claim should be safeguarded.

Because of the church order characteristic of Congregationalism it was necessary to consult each congregation and eventually to secure from it a resolution for the proposed union by 75% of those present and voting at a specially convened meeting. (Such Presbyterians as wished not to unite had to hold such a meeting which would need a 75% vote to withdraw.) The 75% requirement derived, so it was said, from the fact that such a majority is required to alter the rules of a Friendly Society; and a good deal of merriment was caused by the comment of an elderly Congregationalist: 'Our Church is *not* a Friendly Society.' To advocate the scheme and obtain the appropriate consents from all the appropriate levels of church life was a mammoth undertaking for those who were responsible in each of the two Churches; but in the end it was not possible to say that the necessary consultations had not been made and that those involved were not given all the information they needed.

One of the most significant moments in the prolonged discussions in the joint committee was when one of the legal advisers explained that the envisaged union would only be legally possible if the two Churches concerned were prepared to declare that on a certain day each would die and that on the same day a new ecclesiastical being would be brought to birth; for which, as the legal adviser remarked, there seemed to be good scriptural warrant. The fact that in law you cannot simply stick two churchly bodies together with appropriate amounts of ecclesiastical glue was a timely reminder that to achieve Christian unity there has to be a death and resurrection sequence without which the goal cannot be reached.

Such drastic action is not – so far – required by the Ten Propositions, for it is envisaged in these proposals of the Churches' Unity Commission that for the immediate future at least the present denominational structures will remain. It is, nevertheless, worth remembering that no step towards a more visible Christian unity can be taken without sacrifice – not of principle, but of a particular identity which at present hinders the work of the Gospel.

This intermission in the exposition of the Ten Propositions is not included because the writer had a share in the events described in this chapter, but because the formation of the United Reformed Church at least proved that it *is* possible to pass beyond the stage of talking about Christian unity into the fact of it. It can truly be said that as between Congregationalists and Presbyterians there were no such difficulties as are presented by episcopal ordination and establishment of a Church by the state. In that sense it was easier for them to move forward than it was for the Anglicans and Methodists; but it was not *easy*. And the moral most appropriate to the theme of this book is that determined advocacy and constant consultation at every level of Church life are essential if the Christian Churches are to overcome the lethargic conservatism that is the besetting sin of all corporate bodies, Churches not excepted. It is a large matter to find the solution to the theological and ecclesiastical issues which have to be thought through. But that essential part of the contract is relatively easy beside the task of persuading the faithful that they ought to be concerned enough to take action and give consent to those changes which obedience to the Gospel demands.

CHAPTER FOUR

DO WE SHARE THE SAME FAITH?

THE then Archbishop of Canterbury, William Temple, invited the then Principal of Mansfield College, Oxford, Nathaniel Micklem, to write his Lent Book for 1943, *The Doctrine of our Redemption*. In his Preface Dr Micklem took opportunity to remark that the fact of this invitation to a dissenting minister could be taken as an illustration of the fact that 'there is not, and never has been, any dispute between the Church of England and Orthodox Dissent in respect of the articles of the Christian Faith'. The British Faith and Order Conference at Nottingham in 1964 was equally convinced about such agreement, and could see no hindrance to covenanting for union on that ground.

Yet it is necessary to be sure in such grave matters. The General Synod of the Church of England found this to be so when the matter was raised in November 1976. A motion was proposed: 'That this Synod requires that common statements of faith comparable with those agreed with Roman Catholic theologians on the Eucharist, Ministry and Marriage be achieved with the other participating Churches before the practical commitments in the Ten Propositions are entered into.'

This might have been construed as a delaying move, for it would probably have put off the day of decision by at least ten years. That time was greatly shortened by the Archdeacon of Macclesfield who persuaded the Synod that the Churches involved in the Churches' Unity Commission had no doubt doctrinal statements to hand and papers submitted to ecumenical bodies which would make it abundantly clear that the Churches were agreed on the faith. Each of these Churches was accordingly invited to submit appropriate evidence to whatever body in the Church of

England determines these matters.

It remains to be seen what the outcome will be and whether the Archdeacon's confidence will be justified. What is known is that such bodies as the Baptist Union of Great Britain and Ireland, for example, do not have such statements of faith as do most other Christian bodies. They have indeed made doctrinal statements to ecumenical bodies and are members of the Free Church Federal Council which has a very considerable statement of belief; and from time to time various confessions of faith have emerged in Baptist circles, which have been understood as representative of things generally believed among them rather than doctrinal tests to which assent is required. While no one questions the substantial orthodoxy of the Baptist people – as substantial as any other – it is difficult to see how they can provide the sort of evidence that is now expected of them. Does that suggest that the wrong question has been posed? Or that the right question has been wrongly asked?

Gratitude for the Archdeacon's saving amendment was somewhat qualified, however, for those who are to make these submissions by their recollection of recent Anglican history. In 1976 the Archbishops' Commission on Doctrine presented a report, *Christian Believing*, which seemed to show that the puffs of wind raised by changes of doctrine did not disturb the Church of England less than any other. Nor has the General Synod so far considered *Christian Believing* to be an item for its agenda. Was the pot calling in question the colours of the other kettles? But such irritation will not obscure the fact that agreement as to the essentials of the faith is supremely important, and that to move towards unity without some real assurance on this point would be both irresponsible and wrong.

It is not altogether easy to decide what are the *essentials* of the faith and what could be deemed *sufficient agreement*. It is fairly easy to see that to deny any part of the faith would involve exclusion from such agreement; but it is possible, for instance, to assent to the doctrine of the

Blessed Trinity, knowing that there are such different understandings of it that one is driven to ask wherein *sufficient* agreement consists.

It is common to look to the past when such questions are raised, which is right enough within a religion which in all its varied forms looks to the events recorded in Scripture as its starting point and to ancient creeds as its doctrinal standards. Scripture and ancient tradition have a peculiar value for all. Yet we live at a time when history is not greatly valued, doctrinal statements are not much considered, and 'pluralism' is sometimes taken to mean that one theology is as good as another.

Nathaniel Micklem's confident assertion that there 'is not and never has been' any dispute between the Church of England and Orthodox Dissent about the articles of the Christian Faith, is worth more than passing note, because he and the Archbishop for whom he wrote that Lent Book derived from two different traditions in which these matters were differently handled.

The Archbishop, who was not the least adventurous thinker of the day, adhered to a Church which had well-known tests of orthodoxy, the ancient creeds, the Thirty Nine Articles, and the Book of Common Prayer. Together, these represented the body of Anglican divinity. Micklem, however, belonged to the independent element of Orthodox dissent. Confessions of Faith had indeed been made in 1658 and 1833, and he himself helped to compose one in 1966; but these were never used as *tests*. They were representative statements about which a man might say 'yes, in general I stand by that; but I'm not so sure about this or that point'. The attitude of mind represented in this tradition, which is widely reflected in other Free Churches and possibly beyond, derives from a threefold conviction that no form of words can adequately express the fulness of the Gospel, that to require subscription to such statements can lead – and often has led – to restraints upon conscience, and that there are surely other ways of testing the reality of a man's faith than requiring assent to a particular form of words. Holiness of life is as much an evidence of the reality of faith as theological correctness. In holding these convictions the Orthodox dissenters were not careless about doctrine and theology, nor were they lacking in due reverence for scripture and tradition, though they were insistent that tradition should always be judged by the Word of God. They represent an attitude of mind which cannot be overlooked when we consider agreement on the Faith.

Out of two differing traditions these two theologians were essentially at one in doctrine; and it is possible to say that the two traditions which they represented have influenced one another to a considerable degree. The United Reformed Church, for instance, which Micklem lived to see formed in 1972, confessed its faith, declared its thankful acceptance of the witness borne to the Catholic Faith by the Apostles' and Nicene Creeds, and recognized its own particular heritage in such proclamation of faith as its two parent bodies had prepared. But it also declared that 'under the authority of Holy Scripture and in corporate responsibility to Jesus Christ its everliving head', it acknowledged 'its duty to be open at all times to the leading of the Holy Spirit and therefore affirms its right to make such new declaration of its faith and for such purposes as may from time to time be required by obedience to the same Spirit'.

The attitude to historic statements of faith thus expressed, which is not essentially different from that of any Free Church, is not far away in mood from that to be found in the report of the Archbishops' Doctrine Commission on *Subscription and Assent to the 39 Articles* (SPCK 1968). What remains important for all traditions are two questions: how right is it to assume that the categories of thought in which our fathers expressed the faith are normative today? And what expectations do we entertain that the Holy Spirit may make it possible for this or some future generation to make some statement of the Christian Faith which shall be fuller and more adequate than those in earlier times? The faith was indeed delivered once for all to all God's people; to explore and to express the fullness of that 'given' is at once the challenge and the despair of each succeeding generation.

It is thus not difficult to maintain the truth of Micklem's contention. What probably bothers some is that within this apparent agreement there may be disagreement on what any article of the faith may be taken to mean. This comes to its crucial issue, as far as our present theme is concerned, when we come to the clause 'I believe in one holy, catholic and apostolic Church'. To speak of the Church is to be at once involved in discussions about the sacraments and the ministry. We can agree to declare our faith in the Church that it is the Body of Christ, that it is part of the Gospel and not an optional addition to it, that it needs ministry. But we do not all understand the sacraments, or the ministry in the same way. Some speak of the sacrifice of the Mass, while others think more in terms of remembrance. Some speak of the minister as a sacrificing priest, while others think of him as little more than a layman who has had some theological education, to use Paul Tillich's phrase. What does sufficient agreement mean here?

It would be odd indeed if we made 'sufficient' equal to 'exactly the same', for if we did we should have dismissed the great theological controversies of the past and the present as irrelevant and valueless. Arguments about the person of Christ or about the way in which his death and resurrection secure our salvation have evidenced and deepened our understanding of both great doctrines. The clash of ideas has brought illumination. Ought not the same to be true of the doctrine of the Church? Or are those who require to know about such sufficient agreement claiming that to believe in the holy Catholic Church means believing in their understanding of the ministry?

As we explore this sort of question, we need to follow a particular clue and avoid a great danger. The clue lies in the present composition of the Church of England in whose comprehensive embrace reside in relative comfort Christians of very disparate outlooks. At one extreme are those who are more Roman than Rome after Vatican II; at the other some who see theology in similar terms to that of the Southern Baptists. Between these extremes are the majority whose theological colour is very varied. The cynic might poke fun at this comprehension of such variety; but he would be wrong. For here is exemplified par excellence that readiness to hold together those whose apprehension of the same truth is as varied as it is sincere. The creeds may be variously expounded but they are cherished by all; the episcopal ordering of the Church is variously estimated as is the nature of the ministry as a whole, but that ordering is accepted and they are not rejected who differ about the description of the ministry. The comprehensiveness of the Church of England would be destroyed if one party within it insisted that its particular understanding of the atonement, the Church or the ministry were solely acceptable within its life.

This exciting picture of some basic doctrines accepted by all but variously understood prompts the question at what point does comprehension stop? At what point does tolerance have to cry enough? At what point does variety of interpretation appear as denial of the central, basic truth itself? We no longer have heresy trials, for which we may well be thankful. We are so accustomed to pluralism and dialogue that we are apt to blur even proper distinctions. Yet surely there must be a point at which comprehension is stretched so far that it becomes meaningless; otherwise what it comprehends has no distinctive character.

All Churches have to wrestle with this problem; indeed, it involves all Churches as they seek visible unity. It is not possible at this stage to define at what point variety of understanding becomes denial of the central truth; but as we try to follow the clue of comprehension, we had better be aware of the danger, which is ambiguity.

Statements of faith or proposals for unity are sometimes alleged to be ambiguous; but it may well be asked whether such a charge *necessarily* implies fault or dishonesty.

Everything depends, it seems, on the matter being

handled and the motive for making the statement. For example, any six or a dozen clergymen who have that very day recited the Nicene Creed might, if asked, offer as many interpretations of it. This is no cause for wonder, still less for complaint, since the matter in hand is of such infinite meaning that it is inevitable that one man should be particularly aware of one feature and his neighbour of another. Provided that their variety of interpretation arises from the greatness of the theme and that the variety can properly be included within that greatness, all is well. Similarly, if those who in any parish or congregation were asked after a service of Holy Communion what they thought they had been given in it, how it had been given, and what was their own activity during the service, almost as many answers might be forthcoming as there were worshippers. Yet since the worship in which they had been engaged is of such infinite richness, it is more than likely that each was apprehending some part of a glory which none can comprehend.

Ambiguity of this sort is to be expected, since human words and formulae are but frail attempts to describe and witness to what lies far beyond our grasp. The fault comes when words are used to disguise meaning when it is important to know what is being said with some precision. If words are used to paper over a difference which needs further examination and probing, misunderstanding will follow because something less than honest is being said. Rightly or wrongly, the Anglican-Methodist Service of Reconciliation was held to be ambiguous about what in fact would be the consequence of that service for Methodist ministers: were they re-ordained or not? There was at the time variety of understandings, and this at a point where clarity rather than ambiguity was essential. Whether this particular incident is in fact deserving of that comment is in one sense beside the present point, which is that ambiguity is not acceptable in such cases when it is necessary that those involved should have no reason to say 'that was not made clear to us at the time'.

It is against this discussion of sufficient agreement, comprehension and ambiguity that the Ten Propositions are to be studied. In particular attention should be paid to the words of the proposed Covenant. This does not pretend to be a declaration of faith or a complete theological statement, though there is more theology in it than some have noticed! The question to be faced is whether this or something like it provides a sufficient basis on which the Covenanting Churches can agree together on the basis of mutual recognition of memberships and ministries to seek the visible unity of Christ's Church in this land. Does this show and imply sufficient grasp of the Christian faith and do the Churches so recognize one another? And if so, does that recognition derive from an understanding of the Gospel not so much as a possession as a treasure to which we bear witness and by which we ourselves as well as the world are judged?

CHAPTER FIVE

THE COVENANT FOR UNITY

WE have seen that the idea of Churches covenanting together for unity received warm acclaim at the 1964 Faith and Order Conference at Nottingham. But it has to be admitted that as far as most of the British Isles was concerned, the enthusiasm soon waned.

Perhaps some were put off by the target date, 1980, and felt that the sixteen years interval between Nottingham and that scheduled goal-date seemed to envisage too hurried a procedure. Yet in Wales, after much discussion, something happened. In 1975 four of the main Christian bodies in Wales, viz the (Anglican) Church in Wales, the Presbyterian Church in Wales, the Methodist Church and the United Reformed Church, entered into a solemn Covenant for Union, in which they acknowledged each others' fundamental beliefs and practices, and determined to enter on a path of increasing co-operation and common study so as to form, if possible, one visibly united Church out of the four Covenanted Churches. It is to be noted that some Baptist congregations joined the Covenant. Since the Baptist Union has no constitutional right to enter into any such relationship on behalf of its member Churches, this was the only way in which such independent Churches could join the Covenant.

There is obviously a considerable similarity between what has been begun in Wales and what is now contemplated in England; but there are differences, too, which are of some importance. The Welsh Churches covenanted on the basis of an acknowledgement of 'each others' beliefs and practices'. After covenanting they have set up a Commission, which is made up of some twenty-four members officially representing their Churches, together with observers from the other main Churches in Wales.

This Commission is seen as having two tasks. First, there is work to be done in preparing a Scheme for Unity, based on the articles of the Covenant. It is expected that this Scheme will include a full doctrinal statement of Christian belief, and the proposed outline of the United Church in its structure, ministry and modes of action. Second, there is the promotion or commending the proposed union and preparing for it by assessing each Church's resources and initiating common action at national and local levels. At the local level, Area Planning Committees have been set up which are surveying the field of present co-operation and assessing the possibilities of yet more work together.

The main difference between the Welsh plans and the English is clear. In fact, the Welsh started further back, settling only doctrinal issues before covenanting, and setting before them the goal of *organic* unity. In England an attempt is being made to settle more issues before the Covenant is entered into, and the more remote goals are mentioned only in very general terms. No undertaking is made that at the end of the day there will have to be a Scheme of Union, though that is the clear conviction of some. Rather, the Covenant is seen as the opportunity to work for visible unity on the basis of an agreement on faith and on mutual recognition of members and ministries. This step by step approach takes it for granted that to agree to the Ten Propositions is not the end of any road, but the beginning of a journey to a large extent unrouted. At least the goal is in sight; we reach it perhaps in a typically English way, *solvitur ambulando.*

Notwithstanding these somewhat dissimilar objectives, the similarities between the Covenant in Wales and that now under discussion in England are sufficient for it to be instructive for us to look at what Covenant is intended to mean in either case.

The Welsh Covenant, from which the one proposed for England in part derives, is a good deal longer. It begins thus: 'Confessing our faith in Jesus Christ as Lord and Saviour, and renewing our will to serve his mission in the world, our several Churches have been brought into a new relationship with one another. Together we give thanks for all we have in common. Together we repent the sin of perpetuating our division. Together we make known our understanding of the obedience to which we are called.'

Among the items listed in the Covenant are the following: 'We recognize in one another the same faith in the gospel of Jesus Christ found in Holy Scripture, which the creeds of the ancient Church and other historic confessions are intended to safeguard . . . We recognize one another as within the one Church of Jesus Christ, pledged to serve his Kingdom, and sharing in the unity of the Spirit . . . We recognize the members of all our Churches as members of Christ in virtue of their common baptism and common calling to participate in the ministry of the whole Church . . . We recognize the ordained ministries of all our Churches as true ministries of the word and sacraments, through which God's love is proclaimed, his grace mediated, and his fatherly care exercised.'

Then follow these words: 'We do not yet know the form union will take. We approach our task with openness to the Spirit. We believe that God will guide his Church into ways of truth and peace, correcting, strengthening, and renewing it in accordance with the mind of Christ.' It is on this basis that the Covenant rests.

The implications of covenanting are spelt out in a lengthy section only the opening sentences of which need to be quoted here. 'The solemn act of covenanting together before God to work and pray for union should mean that the Covenanting Churches are prepared both to recognize their common membership in the Body of Christ and to act upon it. The Covenant itself, of course, will be only a first step towards union. Although it will be made in the knowledge of the great measure of agreement that already exists between the Churches, difficulties will remain and adequate consideration will have to be given them before full union can be achieved. Nevertheless, it will be as members of a family trusting one another in Christ that the Churches will henceforth view their relationship to one another, rather than as separate entities proceeding along separate ways.' (The full text is available in *Covenanting for Union in Wales*, Part II, 1971, from the Publication Department of the Council of Churches for Wales.)

We may now look more closely at the form of covenant proposed for the Churches in England, though it must be remembered that this form of words is but a draft set down for consideration. It may well be that such Churches as declare themselves willing to covenant with one another may wish to revise the working of the Covenant; but it is unlikely that the general form of it will depart very greatly from what has been suggested.

'We confess our faith in Jesus Christ as Lord and Saviour according to the Scriptures, and acknowledge our calling to serve his mission in the world. We give thanks for all that we have in common; but we recognize that our divisions are an hindrance to that mission. We therefore repent of all that is sinful in our divisions.

Since we recognize in one another faith in the one Gospel of Jesus Christ proclaimed in Scripture, which the creeds of the ancient Church and other historic confessions are intended to safeguard;

And since we recognize one another as within the one Church of Jesus Christ, pledged to serve his kingdom and sharing in the unity of the Spirit;

We therefore pledge ourselves to seek the visible unity of Christ's Church in this land, not yet knowing what form that unity may eventually take, but believing that by taking the steps to which we now commit ourselves we shall be led to a fuller understanding of that unity which is Christ's will for all his people.'

There have been criticisms of this form of words on the ground that it is insufficiently theological. In so far as it uses a good deal of theological shorthand that charge may have some truth in it. But to confess Jesus Christ as Lord and Saviour is something. To recognize in one another faith in the one Gospel of Jesus Christ is something more. To say that this Gospel is proclaimed in Scripture, 'which the creeds of the ancient Church and other historic confessions are intended to safeguard', seems to assent in a nutshell to Trinitarian faith. It would be an unsympathetic critic indeed who found here an implied reduction of the faith.

Assuming, therefore, that the Covenant expresses sufficient agreement in the Gospel, we may remark certain of its features which must be clearly understood if entering into the Covenant is to have full meaning.

Unity and mission describe two indispensable marks of the Church; and there are those who find mission to be of such importance that they regard work for unity as unnecessary. There may have been those who have been so enthusiastic for unity that they have forgotten the call to mission. It is the conviction of those who advocate the Ten Propositions that unity and mission belong together, and that there is real hindrance to mission in disunity. The word of reconciliation cannot be convincingly spoken by those who are manifestly unreconciled.

Those who thus see unity and mission as intimately involved in one another are called upon to be open to the future, to pledge themselves 'to seek the visible unity of Christ's Church in this land, not yet knowing what form that unity may eventually take, but believing that by taking the steps to which we now commit ourselves we shall be led . . .' The pilgrim people are to resume their pilgrimage, to ease themselves from the security of the familiar settlement and risk going on journey with others whom they have known but at a distance. The course of history has given validity to the various forms of the Church with which we are familiar. Good justification can be given to all of them, and frequently is; and to be loyal to one's tradition is no shortcoming. Yet we have to choose whether to perpetuate each tradition in isolation and so retire from the quest for unity or to try to find a way to visible unity which will not deny or jeopardize what is of value in our particular traditions but lead them to mutual enrichment, and, still more, enable us together to discover what in separation must for ever be unknown.

That there are risks in such an undertaking none would deny; but if we are ready to trust one another and seek to be worth trusting ourselves, we could enter into a new stage of Church history. Just as those who enter into the vow and covenant of marriage reach a point at which they are ready to trust one another to face an unknown and uncertain future together, so the Churches are now challenged to say whether they trust each other enough to commit themselves to one another for a similarly unknown and uncertain future. The analogy of marriage must not be pressed too far; but at least it may provide one further indication of how we might proceed. The couple commit themselves to one another on the basis of certain understandings which it is the duty of the minister to ensure that they understand. As far as the proposed Covenant is concerned, those understandings rest principally on the suggested mutual recognition of members and ministries. Are these understandings sufficiently clear and are they adequate for such mutual commitment to set out on the further path towards visible unity?

Naturally enough, there are those who hesitate before taking 'such a risk'; and they argue that since the Christian Churches now get on so much better than they used to about fifty years ago, it will be enough for them to continue in this happier separation. Let them work together whenever possible. Let them worship together so far as they are able; but let them stay much as they are. (On that basis, we should have no sin of disunity of which to be ashamed or of which to repent.)

If the urgencies of local ecumenical projects leave us insufficiently moved to make the sort of reforms which those mission situations require, and indeed if these projects increase rapidly enough in number we may find ourselves in a situation where the normal rules by which

Churches order their lives will be subject to so many exceptions that it will soon be asked why we have the rules at all! Are we unwilling to recognize that the need for our normal rules to be adapted to such important mission circumstances raises some profound questions about those rules themselves? What are we supposed to do when our normal rules obviously injure the work we have been given to do?

The improved Church relations which are so happy a feature of our day could be described as peaceful co-existence. That is indeed far better than the open enmity or unconcealed rivalry which were common enough half a century ago. Yet such co-existence is only a more respectable form of disunity; and it could be called a dangerous luxury, since it at least partially blinds us to the fact that for all our better manners and increased co-operation we are as far as ever from being 'one that the world may believe'.

To covenant on the understanding that there is mutual recognition of members and ministries would be but a beginning on the road towards that form of unity which God wills for his Church; but it would be an important step for the Churches that are ready to take it. There are things which can only be learned after an act of obedience, which could not be learned before. That seems to be one moral to draw from the story of Abraham's setting out 'not knowing whither he went'. But whether the Churches will in fact find the faith and courage so to covenant will in the end depend on whether their love for their Lord and for those who also love and serve him is sufficient to show disunity to be shameful and hurtful. Will the love of Christ constrain us at last to commit ourselves wholeheartedly to one another? That is an important question for English Churches; and not only for them. What is decided in England may well affect what happens in Wales, and elsewhere.

CHAPTER SIX

MUTUAL RECOGNITION OF MEMBERS

WHAT does the Churches' Unity Commission mean when it says in Propositions 4 and 5 that 'we agree to recognize, as from an accepted date, the communicant members in good standing of the other Covenanting Churches as true members of the Body of Christ and welcome them to Holy Communion without condition', and 'we agree that, as from an accepted date, initiation in the Covenanting Churches shall be by mutually acceptable rites'?

To a large extent what is envisaged is already common practice. Methodists and the United Reformed Church, for example, already receive one another's members in exactly this way and their rites of initiation are mutually acceptable. To some extent it is true as between the Church of England and most of the Free Churches. Baptismal rites are not called in question, and communicant members of the Free Churches are welcomed at Holy Communion in the Parish Church on occasion, though if attendance at the Eucharist is to be regular the incumbent is supposed to raise the question of confirmation. Roman Catholics accept baptism in water and in the Triune Name, and in *that* sense recognize the membership of the Catholic Church in all who are so baptized; but there the matter ends, since it is required that those who wish to participate in the life of that Church, particularly in its eucharistic worship, must be confirmed within its discipline.

Whenever Christian initiation is discussed, we need to recall that two patterns of it are familiar within our Churches, and that the merits of each are held and advocated with conscientious vigour. The total process is clear and it includes washing with water and the sharing in the bread and wine: it is baptism reaching its conclusion in the Eucharist.

But at what point should the process begin? Most British Christians are familiar with the pattern of initiation which begins very early in life. An infant is born into a Christian family and very soon is baptized and received into the life of the Church. Thus he is at least set within two spheres of influence: his own family and the Christian family. The Church will make provision for the education of the child in the Christian life, and at whatever is deemed the appropriate moment he is 'prepared for confirmation', or whatever is the appropriate phrase in his part of the Church, so that he may be 'confirmed', thus making his confession of faith in public and being entrusted with the full privileges and responsibilities of membership. Thus he comes to his first Communion. In Churches which follow this pattern of initiation, provision is made, and always has been made, for the baptism of those 'of riper years', who for one reason or another were not baptized as infants. In their case baptism, instruction, confirmation and admission to first Communion will take place within a much shorter space of time.

Other groups of Christians hold different convictions on this important matter. Baptists and Churches of Christ have traditionally opposed Infant Baptism on scriptural grounds. Accordingly, they postpone baptism until the candidate 'knows what he is doing'. The age at which this degree of maturity has been reached will possibly vary very greatly. Some are deemed to have reached it at an early age; others may reach this point of decision a great deal later. It is therefore incorrect to speak of 'Adult Baptism'; 'Believers' Baptism' is the correct description. Churches which hold this conviction do not neglect the Christian education of the children in their midst, and when any person seeks baptism, no doubt he is instructed in the Christian faith and its consequent responsibilities, makes profession of faith, is baptized, sometimes 'confirmed' with the laying on of hands, and received into communicant status. The total process of initiation, therefore, is so to say telescoped into a much shorter space of time than is the case in Churches which practise infant baptism.

Are these two practices of initiation so contradictory of one another that it is impossible to reconcile them? Or is mutual recognition possible?

The CUC has prepared an explanatory note to show how, in its opinion, the mutual recognition of the Churches' members might be arranged. Recognizing that there might properly be a diversity of 'use', it regards as very important that the essential elements of the whole process should be clearly understood. These basic elements may be taken to be five: an appropriate scriptural passage recollecting the events of the life of our Lord to which the Church responds in its rite of initiation; an act of profession of faith and commitment; prayers at the font or baptistery, such prayers to include petition for God's continuing action in the form of the Spirit, that those baptized may be delivered from the dominion of sin into the freedom of the children of God, that buried with Christ they may rise with him to newness of life, and that baptized into the one Body they may share in the one Spirit; the act of baptism by water and in the Threefold Name, with the laying on of hands with the invocation of the Holy Spirit; admission to Holy Communion.

Since in many Christian Churches, Christian initiation is not performed in its entirety at one time, the explanatory note indicates how the progression of the complete rite may be maintained. It shows what may be done at infant baptism and what at the point of confirmation; and it declares that 'where this basic pattern is followed, whether all its elements are administered at one time or at different times, the rites used are such as should be recognized by other Churches and, therefore, are mutually acceptable'. (The note assumes that within the Covenanting Churches those hitherto responsible for presiding at the act of confirmation will continue to do so.)

Would such an understanding of initiation be widely acceptable? Would it 'work'? There are some indications that it might. Two documents in particular indicate that there is a growing consensus that this is the way along which the Churches should develop. *Initiation and Eucharist* (SPCK 1972), by the Joint Liturgical Group, is a document to which CUC is particularly indebted. *One Baptism, One Eucharist, and a Mutually Recognized Ministry*, a report issued by the World Council of Churches in 1975, points in the same direction, and naturally represents a much wider area of consensus. Both these documents would be useful for those who wish to look more deeply into these issues.

It is of special interest to note that two of the Churches participating in CUC (Churches of Christ and United Reformed) are in fact seeking to bridge the baptismal gap at the present time; and the way in which they propose to set about it may be of interest as possibly showing a way which others can follow. The fact is that these two Churches are seeking organic union; but that does not destroy the relevance of their work to our purpose.

The proposal before the two Churches assumes that baptism is the sacrament of entry into the Church and is therefore administered once only to any person. It further assumes that baptism may be administered in infancy or at an age of responsibility, and it expects that both forms of baptism shall be made available in the life of every worshipping congregation. If anyone is baptized at an age of responsibility, upon profession of faith, he at once enters upon the full privileges and responsibilities of membership. If the baptism takes place in infancy, on the profession of faith by the parents, he is placed under the nurture of the Church that he may be led in due time to make his own profession of faith and thus enter upon the full privileges and responsibilities of membership. It is envisaged that within the proposed Church those with differing convictions about baptism shall be included, and both convictions will be honoured. Where these differences of conviction produce tension, it is hoped that they can be pastorally reconciled in mutual understanding and charity. It is provided that 'no one shall be required to administer a form or mode of baptism to which he has conscientious objection, nor shall the form or mode of baptism used in any instance be one to which conscientious objection is taken by the person seeking baptism or by the parent(s) requesting baptism for an infant'.

It is hoped that the Assemblies of the two Churches involved in this proposed organic union will be able to assent to this plan; but however that may turn out, something of that sort will have to be faced by all the Churches if any form of visible unity is to be reached.

However, it is important to note that there are certain problems which need to be solved before all the Churches are able to recognize 'the communicant members in good standing of the other Covenanting Churches as true members of the Body of Christ and welcome them to Holy Communion without condition'.

For some, it is the last words which pose the problem. For example, if a Free Churchman retires to some relatively isolated spot where the Parish Church provides the only easily accessible means of grace, he may, according to the rules as at present, occasionally receive the Holy Communion. If, however, he wishes to do so in a regular way, the local incumbent is expected to raise with him the question of confirmation. It is obviously right that anyone who wishes to be regularly part of another Communion than that in which he has spent most of his life should be asked to make public indication of his readiness to accept the customs and disciplines of his new 'home'. But need that be done in such a way as to separate him from his former companions? Far more important, could not some new rite be devised to welcome a communicant member from another denomination rather than expect him to submit to one which at least appears to suggest that he is becoming a communicant for the first time? 'Without condition' seems to require some such change of custom.

There is no disguising the fact that this Proposition 4 raises serious problems for Baptists, and that on two grounds. The first discloses what at first sight seems an odd fact: a number of Baptists have not been baptized. It is not known for certain how large a number this is, but the fact that there are any at all arises from a conviction held by many Baptists, though not all, that the rite of baptism as such is not as important as the profession of a person's faith in the Lord Jesus. Provided such profession of faith is credibly forthcoming, the rite may follow or may be omitted according to the conviction of the person concerned. Such a person would undoubtedly become a member 'in good standing' in Baptist circles; but could or would other Churches regard him as one whose admission to the Church was 'mutually acceptable'? Would the other Churches – or at least some of them – not require baptism before accepting his membership?

Baptists have often protested against indiscriminate baptism; and many in 'paedo-baptist' Churches (which baptize infants) would support such a protest, and have done and are doing what lies in their power to have this matter better ordered. But what is to happen if one who had been baptized as an infant has drifted away from all real Church life either through the indifference of his parents or because of his own waywardness? At a later point in life some experience reawakens or even for the first time arouses in him true faith. He desires to be baptized, believing that this is the way of obedience for him. But he has already been baptized. It has been the custom among Baptists to baptize such a person, not by way of requiring it of him so much as according to his request; and on the ground of Baptist conviction there seems no reason for refusing baptism. To other Christians, however, it raises very difficult questions indeed, for it amounts to saying that what was done in infancy was no baptism at all; and therefore the word rebaptism is an offence to Baptist ears. It is not enough for the person concerned to say that he knew nothing about his infant baptism and has felt no benefit from it, for an adverse judgement has in fact been passed on the Church and the minister who performed what they believed to be a true sacrament.

Here an impasse of considerable gravity has been reached; but it can be exaggerated, and it is possible to see some ways of easing the problem.

For instance, the person who has come to newfound faith and wishes to be baptized as a consequence could be told that what in some circles is called confirmation – and all Churches have some corresponding rite – could well be the means whereby he makes public profession of his faith and of his commitment to Jesus Christ. Perhaps such a service could – should – be vested with greater significance than it sometimes appears to have.

Lest the issue be seen out of proportion, it needs to be made quite clear that there is no suggestion here that Baptists should abandon believer's baptism. An increasing number of people see this as the proper mode of entrance for those who have not hitherto been baptized; and indeed some who belong to paedo-baptist churches postpone the baptism of their own children so that they may receive it at a time when they can 'decide for themselves'. The question that needs to be put to Baptists is whether they are prepared to accept as true members of Jesus Christ those whose initiation into the fellowship of the Church has followed the paedo-baptist tradition. There seems no doubt that the answer in many cases would certainly be yes, though it needs to be remembered that in Strict Baptist circles the answer would inevitably be much more cautious.

There remain, then, the two questions: what should other Churches do about those members of Baptist Churches who have not been baptized? What should Baptists do about those who have been baptized and wish in more mature years to be baptized again? Is it not possible, one must ask in return, that these cases can be honestly included under Proposition 7, which reads: 'We agree within the fellowship of the Covenanting Churches to respect the rights of conscience, and to continue to accord to all our members such freedom of thought and action as is consistent with the visible unity of the Church.'

CHAPTER SEVEN

MUTUAL RECOGNITION
OF MINISTRIES

IT needs to be remembered all the time that there is a ministry of the whole people of God, and not just a ministry exercised by clergymen. The New Testament makes that plain enough with its description of the gifts of the Spirit which enable *all* Christ's people to fulfil their calling within the body of Christ. Within that whole company there are, however, those who are called to special ministerial service, which is exercised in a representative way; and the special task of this always relatively small group is of leadership in worship and mission, preaching and teaching, pastoral care. Not all these tasks are exclusively the responsibility of the ministry in this specialized and restricted sense; but in any local congregation the leadership normally rests with it.

In the course of Church history various understandings of the ordained ministry have emerged, as is well known. Early in the story there emerged the threefold ministry of bishop, priest and deacon; and this pattern is still to be found, much adapted by the changes of history, in Roman Catholic, Orthodox and Anglican Churches, though it is fair to say that within each of them there are different understandings of these offices. At the time of the Protestant Reformation with the consequent division of Christendom, various patterns of Church order and ministry emerged. As far as England is concerned, there were in the main three patterns.

1. The *Church of England* maintained the threefold ministry and with it the historic succession of bishops. This claim is disputed by Rome; but that does not alter the claim. Nevertheless, the Anglican Church has retained this threefold ministry without having any unanimous under-

standing of it. Some understandings of ministry are 'Catholic', others much more 'Protestant'.

2. Alongside this continuing episcopal ministry, there has emerged the *Presbyterian* type of Church order, in which by a conciliar structure of congregations, presbyteries, synods and assembly a corporate oversight of the Church is exercised by ministers and elders. *Episcope* (Greek for oversight or shepherding) is exercised not by a person (a bishop, *episcopos*) but by corporate bodies at each conciliar level. In that sense it is incorrect to describe these Churches as 'non-episcopal'. Methodists in England have a Presbyterian form of government.

3. More radical still were the *Independents*, whose form of government is followed also by the Baptists. According to them the local church was the universal Church in a nutshell. While each such independent church might well (even should) take counsel with others on all matters which affect their general well-being and on such matters as 'cannot well be otherwise taken up', none has authority over others.

The Churches which fall into any of these types developed their own way of ordaining ministers. Each found its own way of testing the vocation of those aspiring to become ministers, of training them for their future work, and of ordaining them to it. Powerful defences can be and are made of these different methods of ordination; but all of them without exception fail of their intended purpose, with the result that to a certain extent all their ministries are defective. Each, that is, intends to ordain people to the ministry of the universal Church. Ordinations are not to a merely *denominational* ministry. Yet this excellent intention is not fulfilled. Thus the Anglican priest may not exercise his ministry in Roman or Orthodox circles; and the various Free Church ministers may not operate within Anglican circles, still less in Roman and Orthodox. It is true that among the Free Churches there is complete readiness to allow, say, a minister of the United Reformed Church to celebrate the Communion and preach in a

Methodist or Baptist Church; nevertheless he remains a URC minister, under its discipline. He may by courtesy officiate elsewhere; but not of right. This interavailability of ministries in the Free Churches has not of itself been an incentive to union among them, for their determination to be united was never clear.

If ministries are to be mutually recognized, some way must be found of ordaining them in such a way as to secure universal recognition of their ministries; and this, as is notorious, has been the rock on which many schemes of union have been shipwrecked.

But it is not necessary to go into the prolonged history of such schemes and the various difficulties which they encountered, for our business is to look at the proposals made by the Churches' Unity Commission. We shall only make such reference to other schemes as may illustrate this precise theme.

It is suggested that the ordained ministries of all the Covenanting Churches should be recognized as 'true ministries of word and sacraments in the Holy Catholic Church'. This would mean 'acknowledging the reality of the ministries of other Churches', and it is intended that the act of mutual reconciliation and recognition 'would itself bring to all ministries concerned a fulness and a degree of universality which they had previously lacked in separation'. There would, therefore, so it is envisaged, be a service at which this act of reconciliation and recognition would be celebrated, and prayers would be made that God would grant to all the ministries involved 'all the fulness he wishes them to have in the service of Christ in the world'.

Clearly it is not envisaged that these ministers should be 'reordained'. In time past it has often been claimed that those who have not been ordained by a bishop needed so to be brought into the historic succession either by reordination, conditional reordination, or by 'reconciliation', as in the Anglican-Methodist scheme which failed of its purpose in 1972, about which there was some uncertainty whether the Methodist ministers were or were not being reordained. In order to avoid such argument and ambiguity, CUC suggest that all the ordained ministers of such Churches as are ready to covenant should be recognized as true ministers. This has some clear resemblance to what was done at the formation of the Church of South India in 1947: and it is possible to argue that to be brought into communion with the bishop is what is essential rather than 'reordination', which, however it is described, inevitably implies that somehow the one 'reordained' is not a minister in the required sense.

It is true, of course, that to take this line would create an anomaly, that of having those ordained by a bishop serving alongside those otherwise ordained. Yet it could cogently be argued that such an anomaly is not nearly as intolerable as that of Christian disunity. In any case, since the clergy are not immortal, the anomaly would not be eternal!

Care would need to be taken to prepare an appropriate service to celebrate the covenanting of the Churches and the mutual recognition of members and ministries. One point which has been urged upon CUC is that there should be some sign to mark the mutual recognition of ministries. Some have suggested that mutual laying on of hands would be an appropriate sign; but others have argued that this is open to misunderstanding, for an act used in ordination (and on other occasions) would *seem* to have the same meaning at such a service, no matter how solemnly it was declared to have a different meaning. Nevertheless, it is generally agreed that some unambiguous sign would be appropriate; and we may hope that some such will be discovered and agreed upon.

What has been argued thus far in this chapter only makes sense if appropriate arrangements are made about future ordinations. If the Covenanting Churches can accept one anothers' people and parsons by 'mutual recognition', what steps can be taken to ensure that all those ordained after the covenanting will have universal recognition, at least in the sense of recognition by all those Churches?

The Commission suggested that 'all subsequent ordinations to the ministries of the Covenanting Churches shall
be according to a Common Ordinal which will properly
incorporate the episcopal, presbyteral and lay roles in
ordination'.

Not unnaturally the Commission has been asked to
explain in greater detail what is envisaged, and it has replied
that there are, it seems, two ways in which such ordinations
could be conducted.

On the one hand, it would be possible, if they were so
willing, for the Free Churches, i.e. those which at present
do not have bishops, to choose each from its own ministry
those whom it would desire to have as bishops. These would
be set apart to their new office by the ordaining authorities
of all the Covenanting Churches, so that they would receive
from all whatever authority they had to impart. Thereafter
these new bishops would in the areas in their pastoral care
preside at all future ordinations.

Clearly this quite revolutionary step could only be
honestly undertaken if there were on the part of these
Churches a recognition of the fact that such episcopal
ministry is to be seen as 'a visible and significant expression
of the unity and universality of the Church of God'; and
there would be required of them 'a faithful dealing with an
inheritance' and also a 'faithful openness to whatever future
the Lord of the Church intends', which would imply 'a
creative dealing with the inheritance which may hope to
 ...t from it more adequate patterns of episcopal ministry
 ... function and in operation'. Whether Anglican and Free
Churches would be prepared to accept such a proposal
remains to be seen.

On the other hand, it has been argued by some that,
while this acceptance of the episcopate might well be
appropriate and necessary if the goal were *organic* unity,
what we are aiming at in the Ten Propositions is something
short of that, though possibly on the way towards it.

During what might be called the interim period between covenanting and whatever the next stage might be, it would be more appropriate to suggest that ordinations in each denomination should be conducted by whoever normally presides at such a service, and that he should be joined in the act of ordination by those who in the other Covenanting Churches preside on such occasions, the bishop of the diocese being one of them. On this view 'the ministry thus ordained would point forward from the situation of the Churches existing alongside one another towards the discovering of a fuller unity'; and it is argued that this proposal is not concerned only with the act of ordination itself. Within the proposed Covenant, it could lead to the development of ecumenical loyalties and responsibilities. It will 'lead naturally into ever-widening areas of decision-making in common and enable the still separate Churches increasingly to discover their unity in Christ'.

Once again, it remains to be seen whether Anglican and Free Churches will be prepared to accept such a proposal.

The Churches have been asked to say which of these two methods of dealing with future ordinations they prefer; but whichever way that decision goes there will need to be a Common Ordinal.

In accordance with the Commission's view that it is desirable to combine as much variety as is consistent with unity, it is suggested that, provided certain essential elements are common, a good deal of variety is to be welcomed. Those who usually have a simple form of service and those who have a more ornate one should be accepted according to their custom, provided always that these variations do not implicitly or explicitly contradict those elements which are to be held in common.

The general outline of the proposed Common Ordinal is that there should be an agreed Preface. This would not be read at an ordination, but it would stand as a statement of how the Covenanting Churches understand the ministry and what they understand to be done to it at ordination.

The service itself should begin with a service of the word, the presentation and examination of the candidates – the same questions to be asked of all – and an agreed Ordination prayer. Those who normally conduct ordinations in a eucharistic context should continue to do so, knowing that in some traditions this is not customary. By this means a desirable minimum of uniformity would be combined with a considerable amount of variety.

This would apply to the ordinations of ministers (presbyters); clearly similar work will have to be done on the consecration of bishops and the ordination of deacons, for such Churches as retain that order of ministry.

How does the lay role in ordination appear? In at least two places. The selection of candidates for ordination is in all Churches a delicate process and their training is usually a lengthy matter. Lay people have a real share in selection. No candidate can go forward for training without the support of the parish or congregation of which he is a member; and it is not at all impossible that part of his instruction during training should come from a lay person. It would not be unfitting, at the examination of the candidate for ordination, for a lay person to make the appropriate response when the bishop or presiding minister enquires whether such a person is worthy to be ordained. Moreover, when the actual moment of ordination comes there seems good reason for a lay person to lay hands together with the bishop (or presiding minister) and the ministers (presbyters).

'Bishop (or presiding minister)' will look an odd form of words to many. It is used to cover both of the suggestions as to the way in which ordinations in the Covenanting Churches should be conducted. If the non-episcopal Churches become episcopal, the bishop would preside at ordinations; if on the other suggested method, ordinations are, so to say, 'ecumenical' the normal President at ordinations would officiate, assisted by the ordaining officers of the other Covenanting Churches.

Whether these propositions or something very like them

can win the enthusiastic assent of all those concerned remains to be seen; but if the breach between episcopal and non-episcopal Churches is not healed in some satisfactory way the task of discovering visible unity in England will be postponed for many a long year.

It may be worth recalling at the end of this chapter some of the main issues that have to be faced.

In the provisional response to the Ten Propositions from the Roman Catholic Church there is this important sentence. Having said that the Roman Catholic Church in England is not at this time able to take the steps envisaged in Propositions 4, 5 and 6, its representatives nevertheless hope 'that it will prove possible for other Churches to enter this Covenant, as we are convinced that this would notably further the visible unity of Christ's people in accordance with the will of God. Moreover, we see such a step as assisting rather than hindering the relations of these Churches with the Roman Catholic Church.'

It is important to record that statement, since there are many (not all of them within the Church of England) who would regret any step which imperilled their relations with the Church of Rome; and the Canterbury Statement of the Anglican/Roman Catholic International Commission on *Ministry and Ordination* provides material for further discussions in all the Churches.

Yet it is not only about Rome that we need to be sensitive. Free Churchmen, particularly those of the older dissenting tradition, are peculiarly sensitive about bishops. Methodists are on the whole less so, since they did not depart from the Church of England because of conscientious objection to episcopacy, whereas the older Free Churches did. The latter have memories of prelacy, which though now a thing of the past, is still an evocative issue. Moreover, and much more seriously, they have certain convictions about the ordering of the Church on conciliar lines which over the years seem to have shown that bishops are not *necessary* to the life of the Church of God.

For them the issue now is whether the witness of other Christians about the value of the episcopal office is sufficiently persuasive to make it acceptable, not on the grounds of a particular theory about it, but as part of the ordering of the Church which enables it the better to fulfil its vocation.

It is notorious that the whole idea of succession has often been a stumbling-block, if not *the* stumbling-block. Free Churchmen have often been careless about the idea of historical succession; and if they took it seriously they usually argued with such a theologian as P. T. Forsyth that the succession was one of truth. As over against the crude 'pipe-line' theory of succession this argument had its validity, though as stated it could seem more suitable to a university than to a Church. Yet today the idea of succession is set in a much more ample context; and the issue now is whether the Free Churches will be able to see the bishop as one charged with safeguarding the apostolic faith and the provision of care for presbyters and people, to link the ministry to the Church in all places and all ages, and to recognize that it is not a particular theory about episcopacy that is being offered nor a particular pattern of it, but the office itself in the hope that the various Churches, 'learning from one another, may find new patterns of episcopal ministry that will more adequately serve the true ordering of the Body of Christ by the Gospel'.

While it is necessary for Free Churchmen to try to grasp the inwardness of what is understood by the bishop and the historic succession, whether or not they find either acceptable, it is also necessary for Anglicans and Roman Catholics to be especially sensitive about the almost gut reaction of Free Churchmen when asked in Archbishop Fisher's somewhat inelegant phrase to 'take episcopacy into their system'. Are they being asked to deny their history? To go back on all their convictions? Is their conviction about *episcope* exercised through church councils to be set aside? If the propositions are so put to them, a negative response can be guaranteed. If, however, they can be seen as a way by which the characteristic insights and corporate experience of each Church can be honestly blended in such a way that the Church can be more truly ordered and made more fit for mission, then a crucial obstacle may be surmounted.

CHAPTER EIGHT

CHURCH AND STATE

A DISTINCTION is familiar between the Church of England as the established Church of the nation and all the other Churches (including the Roman Catholic) as 'Free' Churches. Yet it conceals the equally important fact that all Churches, and not only the established, are subject to the law of the land.

In quite recent years this has been made clear. The formation of the United Reformed Church in 1972 needed the passage of the United Reformed Church Bill in that year, not indeed to permit the two uniting Churches to unite, but to secure that the properties of the two uniting Churches should become the possession of the new Church, and that those Congregational Churches which had declined to join the United Reformed Church should be justly treated. More recently, the Methodist Church had to undergo parliamentary scrutiny and debate to secure an amendment to the Methodist Church Act of 1929 which would allow the Church to amend its doctrinal standards as and when it seemed right to do so. Churches, then, hold property on terms which the law permits. Their conduct is as much subject to the general laws and customs of the land as anyone else's. They enjoy such privileges as the government accords them and on what terms. Presumably, though this seems extremely unlikely, if some future government were to forbid the further existence of Christian Churches, it could do so; and thereafter such as had the courage to continue as Christians would be outlaws.

Since this is the legal situation, it is necessary to ask at what points the programme outlined in the Ten Propositions would raise issues in which the law would be interested.

Since the Ten Propositions do not envisage in the

immediate future any change in denominational structure, these issues are much less than would have been the case if full-scale organic union were in view. There nevertheless remain some not inconsiderable matters that would need attention.

If, for instance, any number of Baptist Churches wished to join the Covenant, it could well be that their trust deeds would need amendment. Each Baptist Church rests on a trust deed which often contains a doctrinal statement as well as a statement of the conditions on which the property is held and how its affairs may be conducted. If such a trust deed were to state (as some do, though not all) that only those who have been baptized as believers may be members of the Church and/or be welcomed at the Lord's Table, the members of that Church would be precluded from entering the Covenant, unless through the Charity Commissioners the trust deed were amended. This is not mentioned to suggest that all Baptist Churches would be in such a position, since others have more 'open' trust deeds; but it serves as an illustration of the sort of obstacles which a number of Free Churches *might* have to overcome before their intention to covenant for visible unity could be fulfilled.

But what laws of the land would need to be amended to allow a non-episcopally ordained minister to celebrate the Holy Communion in a Parish Church? What legislation would be required to allow a bishop of the Church of England to ordain or to share in the ordination of a non-Anglican minister? There seems good reason to believe that on these two issues at least some amendment of the law would be necessary before covenanting for visible unity could in fact take place; and there may well be other such matters. All that is needful now is to note that such problems will have to be dealt with, and that they may take time and demand much patience. Yet we may be confident that, once the will of the Church has been clearly indicated, the legislators have no desire to frustrate that will.

All this lies in the future; we may hope the not too distant future. There are, however, issues which are nearer to hand.

It will be remembered that in its first report the Churches' Unity Commission listed four features which visible unity would need to display: agreement on a common faith, mutual recognition of members, mutual recognition of ministries, and a readiness to share our worldly goods. The first three of these desirable features found expanded expression in the Ten Propositions, among which the fourth finds no mention. It has not been forgotten, however; and a working group has been set up to consider what legislation would eventually be required to enable such sharing. No one will be surprised to hear that this is a very complicated matter about which those well versed in the law argue considerably; and since the discussion still goes on, it is not possible yet to indicate what the result will be.

But there are two points which can be made with confidence. The first is that we are grateful for the Sharing of Church Buildings Act 1969 which has enabled two important developments. The first concerns those local unions of, say, Methodist and United Reformed Church local churches in places where that has been agreed to be the most sensible way to do the work of the Church. The second concerns those local ecumenical projects in new towns or revamped areas in old towns and cities where it is judged on all sorts of grounds that to set up separate churches would be sinful and wasteful (to some extent sinful because wasteful), and that to share buildings altogether right.

This Sharing of Church Buildings Act 1969 was one of the consequences of the Nottingham Faith and Order Conference of 1964, and it is some indication of progress in ecumenical work to note that the situation envisaged when the act was prepared has noticeably altered even in the short time since it received Royal Assent. There has been a great variety of experiments since the passing of this act; and experience shows that where a Sharing Agreement is used there is already sufficient flexibility to achieve the desired results, always on the assumption that the appropriate denominational authorities are ready to back this or that experiment. The differences in denominational methods of decision-making create difficulties in using the act; yet they have almost always been overcome by goodwill and perseverance.

Nevertheless, it is agreed that the time has come for the ecclesiastical lawyers to consult together to see how far these procedures can be clarified and/or simplified, and also to consider the extent to which this act is in fact capable of much wider reference than has hitherto been understood. Could it be so interpreted as to cover that wider sharing of worldly goods which the Commission sees to be an essential evidence of visible unity? Or would some entirely new legislation be required? At the moment we do not know; but among the items on the agenda of any group concerned with real ecumenical progress it is necessary to keep an eye on what is legally required if the Churches are to move towards closer co-operation and visible unity. None can act as if the state did not exist.

This fact of life which is often and understandably overlooked by ecumenical enthusiasts made it necessary for the Churches' Unity Commission to appoint a working group on the Church-State relationships; and it was encouraged to do so by the Archbishop of Canterbury, who recognized that the present establishment of the Church of England affronts the conscience of many Free Churchmen. While it is true that a large number of the injustices which Roman Catholics as well as other Dissenters suffered from the seventeenth century onwards have now been ameliorated or removed, there remains an important matter of principle: should the Church in any way be subservient or even appear to be subservient to the state? Is it theologically justifiable for the Sovereign to appoint the chief pastors of the Church? It matters little that the Sovereign acts on advice from her ministers; but it is well known that these need not be Christian; and in any case it is the Sovereign, and not the Church, who has the right of appointment.

The Churches' Unity Commission was aware that a debate on this very issue was going on within the Church of England. In 1974 the General Synod of the Church of England went on record as desiring to have a decisive voice in the appointment of its chief pastors. Presumably many had it in mind that after deliberations by those appropriately appointed to the task a nomination should be made direct to the Sovereign. There may have been some who would have gone further; but that would have removed the Sovereign from a significant role in such appointments. The General Synod of 1976 learned that the prime minister had agreed to a new convention. Instead of the task of nomination being the sole responsibility of his office (no doubt after suitable ecclesiastical consultations) he would in future be ready to receive two nominations from the Church, one of which he would recommend to the Sovereign. In the event of his not being satisfied with either of the names thus nominated, he might ask the Church authorities to think again and present further nominations. No doubt the prime minister had in mind the fact that twenty-six of the bishops sit as members of the House of Lords. Was it to be thought that he should have no say in their appointment? If the Church wanted a *completely* decisive voice in the appointment of its chief pastors, would it abandon this position of responsibility and privilege? The General Synod accepted the prime minister's proposed convention and has settled the procedures by which it will discharge its share of the responsibilities now accepted by it.

The Churches' Unity Commission's working group reflected upon this new situation and concluded that, while yet one more step had been taken towards the spiritual liberty of the Church, certain questions still remained. As far as the Free Churches were concerned, what had been agreed by the General Synod seemed a short step in the right direction; but they could not feel that the result was satisfactory. Would the Methodist Church, for instance, consent to present the Sovereign with the names of two possible Presidents of the Conference and happily leave the final choice to Her Majesty?

How does this affect the quest for visible unity which the Churches' Unity Commission is recommending to the Churches? Since the propositions assume that the denominational structures will remain as they are, at least for the time being, it would not greatly affect the main issue if one of the Covenanting Churches were established, with its chief pastors appointed in this way, but if the day should dawn when *organic* unity between the Church of England and any of its other partners were a real issue before them, much more would have to be said. And since by however undefined a route the Covenanting Churches would be working towards visible unity, it may be as well to look at the issue as it now appears to be.

'As it now appears to be' is an important qualification. In the latter part of the last century and the first two decades of the present, such a body as the now defunct Liberation Society existed to set the Church of England free from its bondage to the state. No doubt the pressures which led to the often violent attacks on the establishment were mixed. They arose partly out of the disabilities from which Free Churchmen still suffered. These have now almost entirely been removed and so the reasons for any sense of injustice have thereby disappeared. But there were also profound theological reasons involved in the activities of the Liberation Society; and although by no means all Free Churchmen were supporters of its campaign, they shared its theological convictions. The declaration that 'the Lord Jesus Christ, the only King and head of the Church, has therein appointed a government distinct from civil government and in things spiritual not subordinate thereto, and that civil authorities being always subject to the rule of God, ought to respect the rights of conscience and of religious belief and to serve God's will, justice and peace for all men' may not have been the form in which all Free

Churchmen expressed their convictions on this issue; but they would have certainly agreed to its meaning. The gravamen of their objection to the form of establishment of the Church of England is that it is – or at least seems to be – subordinate to the state, that it is Erastian. The fact that the situation has greatly altered – and from the Free Church point of view greatly improved – in the last half-century only mitigates without altogether removing its fundamental objection.

As the Churches move closer to one another, whether by covenanting or by some other means, the Church-State relationship will have to be discussed and settled in whatever way eventually seems right; and it is of great importance to realize that the position of the Churches on this matter has not remained static. We have already noted how the position of the Church of England has changed; and it is well known that numerous Anglican voices would advocate either disestablishment or some fresh form of establishment. At the same time the mood of the Free Churches has changed, too. While their objections to the present form of establishment remain, they are much less sure that they wish to be rid of all the advantages which flow from establishment of some sort. The Churches, whether established or free, in this country enjoy certain privileges and responsibilities which they would not wish removed. Financial advantages in rating, the ability to reclaim covenanted subscriptions from the Inland Revenue, the privilege of chaplaincies in the services, the hospitals, and places of advanced education, religious instruction in schools – these belong to all the Churches. In *that* sense the Free Churches as well as the Roman Catholics have almost *joined* the 'establishment'.

All this has led a good many in all the Churches to ask whether some form of national recognition might be found which would preserve whatever are the proper advantages of the establishment while dispensing with what are now taken to be its disadvantages. Such a trusted Free Church leader as Dr Ernest Payne gave it as his opinion in 1944 that many Nonconformists were not 'averse to a National Church as such', and therefore were not prepared to press for 'the complete and immediate disestablishment of the Church of England'. Such an attitude found reflection in the opinion of a report of the Free Church Federal Council (1953), that 'though many Free Churchmen reject the state *control* of religion they welcome state *recognition* of religion'.

Since those words were written a great change has come over English life. We have become a multi-racial and therefore a multi-religious community in a way which is quite unprecedented.

The question must therefore be raised how long it is right that one religion, albeit the traditional religion of the land for many centuries, should hold a privileged position at all. One has to ask, whatever the answer turns out to be, whether the fact that no Church is established in the USA has in general terms been worse for religion than the establishment of the Lutheran Church of Sweden has been for the Christians in that land.

It is perhaps a sad reflection that so often the establishment of religion has been discussed in terms of privilege, those who have privilege being sometimes unjust to those who do not have it, and therefore disliked and distrusted on that account. Happily those days are past history, almost completely so. Has the time come when we may turn our minds to think in terms of the responsibilities which the people of God have towards the state? What ought it to be doing for the state and saying to it? Perhaps in the immediate future we may learn how best to define the relationship between Church and state, if we spoke more in terms of responsibility than privilege. That would seem more in keeping with the vision the Lord of the Church gave of service as *the* form of greatness.

The Churches have come much closer together in these past years. We trust that before too long they will come even closer together. Lest in doing so they become more than ever introspective they might include in their responsibility for mission how they should relate to the powers that be. In the end of the day, what matters more than the formal relationship between Church and state (important as that is in itself) is the quality of the influence which the Church as a whole is able to bring to bear on those who determine the quality of the nation's life and the policies which it pursues.

CHAPTER NINE

WHAT NEXT?

WILL anything happen? If it does, what will the results be? No one can confidently answer either question; but they will be asked by many, and a reasoned guess may be worth risking, first remarking that there are two factors in the current situation which some may all too easily overlook.

Whether to covenant with the other Churches poses for all concerned some profound and important theological and ecclesiastical questions. No doubt all those qualified to deal with such matters will express their judgements and help those less able to see what the crucial points are. Equally without doubt those whose enthusiasm rests on prejudice rather than reason will be equally if not more eloquent. It is to be feared that their voices will be well heard. So it will all be taken with great seriousness – by a few. The man on the top of a bus at Clapham Common will not bother either way. If the Covenant is entered into, he may notice a headline in the evening paper, as he turns to whatever page is most likely to reflect his real interest. For the great majority of Christian people in this country the discussion is about non-questions. The questions which vex the minds of the Churches' Unity Commission and those who eagerly discuss its propositions are not those which trouble their minds. An earlier chapter was an attempt to show why the questions of Church order and the like are at their own level of vital importance; but it is a fact that most Christians simply do not see why 'the Churches don't get on with it'. Life is too urgent and important to bother with ecclesiastical 'niceties'. The theologians and ecclesiastics cannot agree with that; but they had better not forget that while the top-brass debate this is the mood of the troops.

Among the Christian people who will be most affected by Church decisions about visible unity will be those who work in local ecumenical projects, of which there are now 289 in England. These are, as it were, frontier mission stations in modern society in which Christians of more than one tradition are persuaded that it is for all sorts of reasons better to conduct their work unitedly rather than in division. Few can be heard to regret such action, and most rejoice greatly to know that at least somewhere something is 'being done' about unity. But the problems of such enterprises do not go away because they have, so to speak, been left on one side in this locality. Sooner or later youngsters and others need to be confirmed. Joint confirmations are frequently arranged, so that those thus admitted to the full privileges and responsibilities of the Church belong to that ecumenical parish in all its 'parts'. In a mobile society they will before long move to others areas in which – God pardon us for our sins! – Church life is more 'normal', and they will have to decide which Christian 'label' to wear. All they wanted was to be Christian; and there are severe words spoken about those who put stones of stumbling in their path. Those who work in these local ecumenical projects frequently say that they know the urgency of visible unity but that the problems cannot be settled at the local level. Some national decisions are required. If they are not made, those who work in these spheres will still have to wrestle with their intractable problems about denominational demarcations, still have to cope with the problems that arise when ministries are not mutually recognized, still have to cope with the frustrations of their young folk who are puzzled and put off by the divisions in the Church which mean nothing to them.

Of course, we cannot move towards visible unity just because of the urgent impatience of those who work where the shoe is pinching; but as we make our decisions let us not forget that not all Christians live in suburbs or villages where it is fairly easy to say 'we can go on as we are a bit longer yet'.

With that sort of bewildering background to the decisions which will need to be made before too long, what are the prospects?

Much depends on which of the participating Churches decide to covenant, and it would be folly and impertinence to forecast which they will be. But some possible contingencies can be foreseen.

It is impossible to exaggerate the importance of the decision taken by the Church of England; and it is greatly to be hoped that it will be able so to covenant in ways with which at least some of the Free Churches will be happy to agree. If for whatever reason it fails to do so, then the movement towards unity will be given perhaps the most serious setback it could receive in this land; and the consequences of that failure are hard indeed to reckon. One might well fear that other Churches would feel too discouraged to make any further attempts to unite with it for a good many years to come.

There is, however, no need to assume that this disastrous course will be followed; and it is well known that a great many within the Church of England are making serious efforts to see that the propositions are known and understood, and are doing their utmost to see that the hoped for answer is given.

That said, Free Churchmen need to remember the Anglicans' sense of historical development and tradition, their anxiety lest the comprehensiveness of their Church should be fatally disturbed, their responsibility to the nation for the nation's well being. It may be argued, of course, that to some extent all Churches share these concerns also; what needs to be discovered is whether we can share them in such a way as to be seen to share them. There can be few Anglicans who nowadays think of the road to visible unity as a one-way traffic filled with those who are coming back to the home they deserted all those years ago. What needs to be made clear is whether the Church of England and its 'separated brethren' can somehow be gathered into the sort of Church that will include all the truth and value about which their fathers so disagreed that they parted company.

It cannot be taken for granted that the Free Churches will decide to covenant, though it is often assumed that they will be easier to persuade. That they wish for greater unity there can be no doubt; but they will examine the episcopal role in ordination with more than usual care. Denominational pride and the self-consciousness of being comparatively small in number will combine to make them sensitive about being 'taken over' or 'swallowed up'. Yet among them also are those who work hard at preparing for what they hope will be a positive answer to covenanting.

If all goes well and several of the eight participating Churches agree to covenant, then we might expect that the impetus of such a decision might arouse many to work more zealously in the new context. Certainly Christian co-operation would become infinitely easier because at long last it would have become more natural; and the fact that all had in their own way made a big decision would enable our eyes to be sufficiently opened to see to what next step God is calling his people.

In the unhappy event of the Church of England not being able to covenant, it may be assumed that at least two of the Free Churches, possibly more, would have agreed to do so. About that outcome few Free Churchmen would be keen. The Methodist and United Reformed Churches would more or less be obliged to unite, since so many of their local congregations have already done so; and in fact these two denominations have held back from direct negotiations with each other until the final decisions about the Ten Propositions have been made, believing that something bigger than union between them alone is what is now needed. There are many who would regard the creation of what would inevitably look like a Free Church *bloc* as a poor second-best; and they would regret it all the more since they might have to live with it for some years to come.

Supposing that all goes as well as ever possible -- whatever that may be! – we already know that the Roman Catholic Church will not be able to covenant 'at this time'; and that throws into sharper relief the tenth Proposition: 'We agree to remain in close fellowship and consultation with all Churches represented on the Churches' Unity Commission.' The Roman Catholic provisional response to the Ten Propositions welcomes this intention to increase collaboration in the search for unity with those who are able to covenant. This is to be taken together with their readiness to examine 'the possibility of suitable forms of covenant at local level'. This could well be seen as a means of expressing 'the seriousness of the commitment to unity already voiced in the official teaching of the Church'.

It is of the greatest importance that those who have been brought together in the Commission should remain together, though it is not yet clear what form their fellowship and consultation could best take. The Roman Catholic presence has been so welcome, and its contribution to the Commission's work so valuable, that it seems indispensible to our fellowship in the future.

But what of those Christian communities beyond the bounds of the Commission – the Quakers, the Salvation Army, the whole army of Pentecostal Churches of whatever colour? That we cannot as yet foresee; but we can be confident that as the Churches move forward to closer unity and as the goal which God has set before us becomes more clearly defined, we shall find that these partners in Christ are not farther from us than they are at present. Indeed, we hope that the way may be found for them to become more and more closely related to the Covenanting Churches, and that their unity with us will become increasingly visible.

This brief concluding chapter is written 'as seeing through a glass darkly'. It may be that the future will be brighter than our fears allow us to hope, or that it will be darker than our worse fears counsel us to dread. What is clear is that in the immediate future decisions must be made as a result of which the shape of that future will be to a large extent settled. We must realize that what we are asked to take is but an initial step on what may well be a long journey; but in one sense the first step is the most important, since without it there can be no more.

APPENDIX A

THE following quotations serve to show some of the stages by which the English Churches have reached their present quest for visible unity. The dates of these statements indicate how long the quest has so far taken.

1920   THE LAMBETH CONFERENCE

The times call us to a new outlook and new measures. The Faith cannot be adequately apprehended and the battle of the Kingdom cannot be worthily fought while the body is divided, and is thus unable to grow up into the fullness of the life of Christ. The time has come, we believe, for all the separated groups of Christians to agree in forgetting the things which are behind and reaching out towards the goal of a reunited Catholic Church. The removal of the barriers which have arisen between them will only be brought about by a new comradeship of those whose faces are definitely set this way.

The vision which rises before us is that of a Church, genuinely Catholic, loyal to all truth, and gathering into its fellowship all "who profess and call themselves Christians", within whose visible unity all the treasures of faith and order, bequeathed as a heritage by the past to the present, shall be possessed in common, and made serviceable to the whole Body of Christ. Within this unity Christian Communions now separated from one another would retain much that has long been distinctive in their methods of worship and service. It is through a rich diversity of life and devotion that the unity of the whole fellowship will be fulfilled.

This means an adventure of goodwill and still more of faith, for nothing less is required than a new discovery of the creative resources of God. To this adventure we are convinced that God is now calling all the members of his Church.

We believe that the visible unity of the Church will be found to involve the whole-hearted acceptance of:

The Holy Scriptures, as the record of God's revelation of himself to man, and as being the rule and ultimate standard of faith; and the Creed commonly called Nicene, as the sufficient statement of the Christian faith, and either it or the Apostles' Creed as the Baptismal confession of belief:

The divinely instituted sacraments of Baptism and the Holy Communion, as expressing for all the corporate life of the whole fellowship in and with Christ:

A ministry acknowledged by every part of the Church as possessing not only the inward call of the Spirit, but also the commission of Christ and the authority of the whole body.

The various Free Churches replied with gratitude for the spirit of Lambeth Appeal to All Christian People, but indicated the difficulty they all felt about episcopal ordination and the spiritual freedom of the Church.

1938 OUTLINE OF A REUNION SCHEME

This scheme is drafted in the belief that it is the will of God that in this world the spiritual unity of his Church should be manifested in a visible society, holding the one faith, having its recognized ministry, using God-given means of grace and inspiring all its members to the world-wide service of the Kingdom of God.

It rests upon the conviction that the unity of the Church is involved in the Christian Doctrine of God, and is demanded for the manifestation and achievement of his purpose. As there is one Lord, one Faith, one Baptism, one God and Father of us all, so there must be one Body, one fellowship of the people of God on earth, seen of all men; for it is the purpose of God not only to reconcile all men through Christ to himself, but also to unite them to one another in the Body of Christ.

The divisions among Christian people everywhere disable them from serving God according to the will of Christ and obstruct his purpose to win and rule over men.

This disunion debars us from giving our torn and distracted world effective witness to the truth that the Gospel of Christ is the one basis of enduring fellowship among men and nations. Similarly it confuses and weakens the presentation and imperils the acceptance of our Christian message, especially in the mission field. The continuance of this disunion involves a waste which is sinful inasmuch as it hinders the work of God.

Our ideal of reunion is one of unity with variety. It does not mean absorption by any existing body, nor would it involve a flat and meagre uniformity; rather it would conserve, and make more widely available, the spiritual treasures at present cherished in separation. The spiritual vitality of each section suffers through isolation in organisation from the rest. While the value of the present varieties of emphasis in Christian faith and experience must be preserved, these very varieties should be varieties within the life of one Body.

This scheme makes its own the ideal set forth by the Lambeth Conference of 1920, and reaffirmed by the Lambeth Conference of 1930.

In every effort to bring together divided members of Christ's Body the final aim must be the union in the Universal Church of all who acknowledge Christ as Lord, and the test of all local schemes of union is that they should express locally the principle of the great catholic unity of the Body of Christ.

The united Church of England (a) desires in no way to impair the fellowship and communion which the constituent bodies from which it has been formed have previously enjoyed in England and throughout the world, and (b) will continually work towards the goal of the full union in one body of all parts of the Church of Christ.

1946   ARCHBISHOP FISHER'S CAMBRIDGE SERMON

There is a suggestion which I should like in all humility to make to my brethren of other denominations. We do not desire a federation: that does not restore the circulation. As I have suggested, the road is not yet open, we are not yet ready for organic or constitutional union. But there can be a process of assimilation, of growing alike. What we need is that while the folds remain distinct, there should be a movement towards a free and unfettered exchange of life in worship and sacrament between them as there is already of prayer and thought and Christian fellowship – in short that they should grow towards that full communion with one another, which already in their separation they have with Christ . . .

My longing is, not yet that we should be *united* with other Churches in this country, but that we should grow to full *communion* with them. As I have said and as negotiations have shown, no insuperable barrier to that remains until we come to questions of the ministry and government of the Church. Full communion between Churches means not that they are identical in all ways, but that there is no barrier to exchange of their ministers and ministries. Every Church's ministry is effective as a means by which the life of Christ reaches his people. Every Church's ministry is defective because it is prevented from operating in all the folds of his flock. For full communion between Churches there is needed a ministry mutually acknowledged by all as possessing not only the inward call of the Spirit but also the authority which each Church in conscience requires.

At the Lausanne Conference of Churches in 1927, it was said that in view of the place which the Episcopate, the Council of Presbyters, and the Congregation of the Faithful respectively had in the constitution of the early Church, in view of the fact that these three elements are each today and have been for centuries accepted by great Communions in Christendom, and that they are each believed by many to be essential to the good order of the Church, "We recognize that these several elements must all . . . have an appropriate place in the order of life of a reunited Church". Every constitutional scheme has proceeded on those lines. The non-episcopal Churches have accepted the principle that episcopacy must exist along with the other elements in a reunited Church. For reasons obvious enough in Church history, they fear what may be made of episcopacy. But they accept the fact of it. If they do so for a reunited Church, why not also and earlier for the process of assimilation, as a step towards full communion? It may be said that in a reunited Church they could guard themselves in the constitution against abuses of episcopacy. But they could do so far more effectively by taking it into their own system. The Church of England has not yet found the finally satisfying use of episcopacy in practice: nor certainly has the Church of Rome. If non-episcopal Churches agree that it must come into the picture, could not they take it and try it out on their own ground first?

It is not of course quite as simple as all that. There are requirements and functions which Catholic tradition attaches to the office of a bishop in the Church of God, which, if our aim is assimilation and full communion, must be safeguarded. Negotiators in the past have been able to agree upon them, and could with hope enquire into them further, if our non-episcopal brethren were able to contemplate the step I suggest. As it seems to me, it is an easier step for them to contemplate than those involved in a union of Churches: and if achieved, it would immensely carry us forward towards full communion, without the fearful complexities and upheavals of a constitutional union. In such a giving and receiving of episcopacy, there would be a mutual removal of a barrier between the folds. Nor would any fresh barriers be raised, such as may be by a constitutional scheme. For no previous existing affiliations would be impaired.

1950   EXTRACT FROM A REPORT OF CONVERSATIONS BETWEEN REPRESENTATIVES OF THE ARCHBISHOP OF CANTERBURY AND OF THE EVANGELICAL FREE CHURCHES IN ENGLAND

There have been in the past many Free Churchmen who have strongly held that their Church Order must conform to a pattern set out in Scripture. In the seventeenth century that was the view of both Presbyterians and Independents. It is still the view of some. Many more would hold the view that their so-called non-episcopal order is closer to that of the early Church than the developed episcopal order, and therefore to be preferred. On the other hand, most Anglicans would probably still adhere to the view of Hooker that episcopacy is a legitimate and expedient development from primitive Church Order, while even those who would seek for a definite authority for episcopacy in Scripture would admit that there have been very great changes in the way in which the episcopate has functioned. They will also admit that changes will and should continue . . .

We do not need here to discuss in any detail all the matters which, in the course of the centuries, have been associated with the subject of Church Order. The broad distinction appears in our midst between those Churches which maintain a separated order and succession of bishops, and those which are without such an order (or, if they possess one, as in the case of the Moravians, do not regard it as a necessary form of Church Order). The Anglican Church stands for the maintenance of an episcopal succession, whether or not it can be traced back to apostolic times, as a link with the ministry of the ancient Church and an expression and safeguard of the unity and universality of the faith . . .

Our special task has been to consider whether the Free Churches of this country could "take episcopacy into their systems" in such a way as to make intercommunion poss-ible; and, if so, exactly what this step would involve both for Free Churchmen and Anglicans. In South India episcopal and non-episcopal churches have united on an episcopal basis. In Ceylon a somewhat similar scheme is projected. We recognize, however, as did the Archbishop in his sermon and the Anglican bishops in their meeting at Lambeth in 1948, that the English situation is one of peculiar difficulty and complexity.

The Free Churches have had a long-standing and deeply-felt suspicion of episcopacy in its traditional Anglican form. They reacted from it in the form it took after the Eliza-bethan religious settlement, their case against it resting on their study of the New Testament and their understanding of the Gospel. What many of them suffered at the hands of the bishops from the late sixteenth to the early nineteenth centuries explains, if it does not justify, the attitude they have often adopted to an episcopal order of ministry as such. They are assured that, though non-episcopal in their Church Order, they have had the blessing of God on their witness and have known the presence of the Lord and the power of the Holy Spirit in their sacramental worship and their Church fellowship. It is clear to us all that the history of the past three hundred years cannot be wiped out, or treated as if it did not exist, and that episcopacy cannot be offered to or accepted by the Free Churches as a mere matter of expediency or in a completely undefined form. Moreover, the attitudes taken by the Roman Church and the Orthodox Churches to one another, and to the Orders of the Church of England, are a check to extravagant claims for episcopacy as such. It has not always secured or guaran-teed the unity, continuity, or apostolic faith of the Church, though it has borne witness to them.

The question before our Churches is whether, for the sake of greater visible unity, for the sake of a swifter and surer growing together of the separated Christian traditions, and for the sake of eucharistic fellowship, which is at present impossible, the link with the historic succession of bishops, which is preserved by the Church of England, should be accepted by the Free Churches; whether this can be done without the abandonment of either side of vital principles; whether, even if some ambiguities still remain, the spiritual advantages for all would manifestly out-weigh the difficulties which would have to be faced and overcome.

Much would clearly depend on the way in which this acceptance of the historic episcopate and its likely consequences were presented to the Churches. We are certain that the necessary conviction and enthusiasm would be forthcoming only where, in addition to the acceptance of the principle set out above, it is recognized both by Anglicans and Free Churchmen that Bishops form but one part of the Ministry of the Church and must have associated with them Presbyters as well as those usually designated the laity.

For the Free Churches it would be a further essential principle that they should remain free to maintain the relations of fellowship and intercommunion which they at present enjoy with non-episcopal Churches.

1952/3 REPORT OF THE BAPTIST UNION OF GREAT BRITAIN AND IRELAND ON CHURCH RELATIONS IN ENGLAND

The question before us is whether there could be Baptist Bishops, linked in the manner suggested with the episcopal successions of the past and exercising the functions mentioned above.

Any such step would undoubtedly be a departure from the traditional emphasis expressed in our church order and found at present in all the Baptist communions throughout the world. That such a departure would be involved might not in itself justify our rejection of the proposals. But since, in our opinion, acceptance would jeopardize some of the cherished convictions on which we build and which we believe we hold in trust for the whole Church, it is necessary for us frankly to state the difficulties and objections as we see them. While we do this, however, we would, at the same time, insist that with others we also are alive to the need for all Christians to draw together, and, if possible, in intercommunion. Such an intimacy of fellowship is necessary that all Christians may realize our Lord's own thought and prayer as given in the New Testament, and that Christians may make a more effective witness against the secularity of the world. The Church, as described in the New Testament, is one and indivisible. Its oneness, we agree, ought to be more clearly expressed in unity of worship and service, till the conditions of earth are more fully a reflection of conditions in heaven. This is our view, as indeed it is bound to be the view of all earnest disciples of our Lord – ours and theirs . . .

We cannot believe that intercommunion between Christian Churches should be made dependent upon episcopacy. A properly authenticated and recognized ministry there should be, but this does not in our view depend upon having a special order of bishops. We believe that before there can be satisfactory progress towards intercommunion in this country the claims made on behalf of the present Free Church ministries must be more properly recognized. It is admitted in the report that if the proposals before us were adopted, in the early stages at least, "grave difficulties would be involved in the existence of two types of minister within a single Church", those who had received episcopal ordination and those who had not, and that the Church of England would allow its members to receive the sacrament of Holy Communion at the hands only of such ministers of the Free Church as had been consecrated to the episcopate or episcopally ordained. This would result in a situation which would be, in our opinion, quite unacceptable, indeed intolerable . . .

Baptists regard ordination as a function of the whole Church acting through the fellowship of the local church. The local company of believers after seeking the guidance of the Holy Spirit chooses those who have received gifts for special office. The actual ordaining is in our view of

God, even as the ministry is a ministry under God for the edification of the Church, i.e. the Church as a whole. The service is the public acknowledgement in the Church that a candidate has been called of God to the work of the ministry. To say that someone must of necessity by virtue of his office take part in such a service because, if he does not, there will be no regular or proper ordination would be to introduce a new and alien element, a legalistic and coercive element, into our church life. We believe that an ordination cannot take place except in and through the fellowship of Christian people; but that fellowship is more important than the presence and act of any individual, whatever his status or title.

1952   THE METHODIST CHURCH'S RESPONSE TO CHURCH RELATIONS IN ENGLAND

... the Archbishop's proposals imply that Intercommunion could be achieved only if the Free Churches accepted an episcopate "consecrated in the first instance through Bishops of one or more of the historic episcopal Churches and thus linked with the episcopate of the past, and would adopt episcopal ordination as its rule for the future". This requirement is of crucial significance and we believe that it should be examined in the light of the following considerations:

i) We would call attention to a declaration of the Methodist Conference of 1939: "The Methodist Church does not claim that either episcopacy or any form of organization even in the Apostolic Church should be determinative for the Church for all time. It would not be able to accept episcopacy and episcopal ordination if such acceptance involved the admission that either of these is indispensable to the Church" . . . "Again, the Methodist Church is unable to accept the theory of Apostolic succession interpreted as the succession of Bishops in the principal sees of Christendom, handing down and preserving the Apostles' doctrine and regarded, as in certain Churches it is regarded, as constituting the true and only guarantee of sacramental grace and right doctrine." By this declaration the Methodist Church stands and we have reason to believe that it would receive the assent of many Anglicans.

ii) In considering the proposal of the Archbishop that non-episcopal Churches might take episcopacy into their systems the Committee would distinguish between episcopacy and those episcopal functions which are inseparable from the corporate life of the Free Churches as well as the Church of England. The Methodist Church has various organs for the fulfilment of episcopal functions as described in the Report:

(a) Ordination.

(b) Decision in concurrence with Presbyters and Laity in any suggested changes in matters of doctrine.

(c) Pastoral oversight of Ministers and congregations.

These functions have been and are exercised in British Methodism independently of episcopacy and episcopal succession. Further, we believe that non-episcopal as well as episcopal systems have been divinely used to express and safeguard the Apostolic Gospel. By the preaching of the Word, the due administration of the Sacraments, the care exercised in the ordination of Ministers to their sacred office as Ministers of the Church of God, the varied ministries of the laity, the fellowship of believers in the quest for holiness and in world evangelization, the Methodist Church has been concerned to preserve unity and continuity of witness to the Catholic faith. Hence it is not possible for Methodism without betraying its own heritage to share the conviction which seems to be without warrant in the New Testament that episcopacy is essential to the life of the Church and that non-episcopal Ministries are gravely defective, even if it is readily admitted that they bear the fruits of the Spirit and have been richly blessed by God.

1955   CONVOCATION OF CANTERBURY

Resolution passed in both Houses on Church Relations in England. (A similar resolution was passed on the same day by the convocation of York.) To these the Methodist Church responded and the negotiations between the two Churches began.

1964   DECREE ON ECUMENISM OF VATICAN II

Article 1 : The restoration of unity among Christians is one of the principal concerns of the Second Vatican Council. Christ the Lord founded one Church and one Church only. However, many Christian communions present themselves to men as the true inheritors of Jesus Christ; all indeed profess to be followers of the Lord but they differ in mind and go their different ways, as if Christ himself were divided. Certainly, such division openly contradicts the will of Christ, scandalizes the world, and damages that most holy cause, the preaching of the Gospel to every creature.

The Lord of Ages nevertheless wisely and patiently follows out the plan of his grace on our behalf, sinners that we are. In recent times he has begun to bestow more generously upon divided Christians remorse over their divisions and longing for unity.

Everywhere large numbers have felt the impulse of this grace, and among our separated brethren also there increases from day to day a movement, fostered by the grace of the Holy Spirit, for the restoration of unity among all Christians. Taking part in this movement, which is called ecumenical, are those who invoke the Triune God and confess Jesus as Lord and Saviour. They do this not merely as individuals but also as members of the corporate groups in which they have heard the Gospel, and which each regards as his Church and, indeed, God's. And yet, almost everyone, though in different ways, longs for the one visible Church of God, a Church truly universal and sent forth to the whole world that the world may be converted to the Gospel and so be saved, to the glory of God.

The sacred Council gladly notes all this. It has already declared its teaching on the Church, and now, moved by a desire for the restoration of unity among all the followers of Christ, it wishes to set before all Catholics guidelines, helps and methods, by which they too can respond to the grace of this divine call.

Article 3: ... some, even very many, of the most significant elements and endowments which together go to build up and give life to the Church itself, can exist outside the visible boundaries of the Catholic Church: the written Word of God; the life of grace; faith, hope and charity, with the other interior gifts of the Holy Spirit, as well as visible elements. All of these, which come from Christ and lead back to him, belong by right to the one Church of Christ.

The brethren divided from us also carry out many liturgical actions of the Christian religion. In ways that vary according to the condition of each Church of community, these liturgical actions most certainly can truly engender a life of grace, and, one must say, can aptly give access to the communion of salvation.

It follows that the separated Churches and communities as such, though we believe they suffer from the defects already mentioned, have been by no means deprived of significance and importance in the mystery of salvation. For the Spirit of Christ has not refrained from using them as means of salvation which derive their efficacy from the very fullness of grace and truth entrusted to the Catholic Church.

Nevertheless, our separated brethren, whether considered as individuals or as communities and Churches, are not blessed with that unity which Jesus Christ wished to bestow on all those to whom he has given new birth into one body, and whom he has quickened to newness of life – that unity which the holy scriptures and the ancient tradition of the Church proclaim. For it is through Christ's Catholic Church alone, which is the universal help towards salvation, that the fullness of the means of salvation can be obtained. It was to the apostolic college alone, of which Peter is the head, that we believe that Our Lord entrusted all the blessings of the New Covenant, in order to establish on earth the one Body of Christ into which all those should be fully incorporated who belong in any way to the people of God. During its pilgrimage on earth, this people, though still in its members liable to sin, is growing in Christ and is guided by God's gentle wisdom, according to his hidden designs, until it shall happily arrive at the fullness of eternal glory in the heavenly Jerusalem.

Article 4: Today, in many parts of the world, under the influence of the grace of the Holy Spirit, many efforts are being made in prayer, word and action to attain that fullness of unity which Jesus Christ desires. The sacred Council exhorts, therefore, all the Catholic faithful to recognize the signs of the times and to take an active and intelligent part in the work of ecumenism . . . Catholics must gladly acknowledge and esteem the truly Christian endowments for our common heritage which are to be found among our separated brethren. It is right and salutary to recognize the riches of Christ and virtuous works in the lives of others who are bearing witness to Christ, sometimes even to the shedding of their blood. For God is always wonderful in his works and worthy of all praise.

Nor should we forget that anything wrought by the grace of the Holy Spirit in the hearts of our separated brethren can contribute to our own edification. Whatever is truly Christian is never contrary to what genuinely belongs to the faith; indeed, it can always bring a more perfect realization of the very mystery of Christ and the Church.

Nevertheless, the divisions among Christians prevent the Church from realizing the fullness of catholicity proper to her in those of her sons who, though joined to her by baptism, are yet separated from full communion with her. Furthermore, the Church herself finds it more difficult to express in actual life her full catholicity in all its aspects.

1967 BAPTISTS AND UNITY

It is in the local church that Baptists find their Christian life centred. Within it they are nurtured and come to a confession of faith in baptism. Within it they find themselves as members of a fellowship of believers. Within it and through it they share in the responsibility of Christians in mission to the world. All too often, however, Baptists, whilst being deeply concerned for particular mission work on the traditional mission fields abroad, have insufficient concern for the sense of wholeness of the Christian Church either in extent or in unity.

Whilst there is no doubt that it is in the local church that church membership becomes meaningful, and that the local church is a company obviously engaged in mission, to have insufficient regard for the wider fellowship is to be deficient in churchmanship, according both to the New Testament and also to the stated Baptist understanding of the Church. We would call attention to two statements, both taken from the declaration issued in 1948:

"Although Baptists have for so long held a position separate from that of other communions, they have always claimed to be part of the one, holy, catholic Church of our Lord Jesus Christ. They believe in the catholic Church as the holy society of believers in our Lord Jesus Christ, which he founded, of which he is the only Head, and in which he dwells by his Spirit, so that though manifested in many communions, organized in various modes and scattered throughout the world, it is yet one in him." "It is in membership of a local church in one place that the fellowship of the one, holy, catholic Church becomes significant. Indeed, such gathered companies of believers are the local manifestation of the one Church of God on earth and in heaven. Thus the church at Ephesus is described, in words which strictly belong to the whole catholic Church, as 'the church of God, which he hath purchased with his own blood' (Acts 21:28). The vital relationship to Christ which is implied in full communicant membership in a local church carries with it membership in the Church which is both in time and in eternity, both militant and triumphant. To worship and serve in such a local Christian community is for Baptists, of the essence of churchmanship."

If Baptists really believe these statements there is clearly contained within them a challenge to face up to the events of today. For the visible unity of Christ's Church is a concept rooted in the New Testament and we cannot, as true followers of Christ, ignore what the Spirit is doing in the churches today. Do any of us really believe that it is not the Spirit of Christ who is drawing churches out of isolation into discussion and activity together? The realities of the Church's unity that have engaged our attention surely demand that some effort be made to embody them in the empirical life of the Church; is it really God's will to cease such efforts and leave the appalling *status quo* till the Second Coming of Christ and the Last Judgement? And what will the Judge say to us if we do? If the unity of the Church is of moment to him, ought it not to be of concern to us? It is clear that opinions differ as to how the Church's unity is to be known and expressed; such difference calls for participation in the discussions that are proceeding among the churches, that we may together learn the mind of the Spirit for the Church today.

1970   GROWING INTO UNION

(Buchanan, Mascall, Packer and Leonard)

Proposed form and manner of ministerial Integration.

Preface to the Ordinal
(The first paragraph would describe the continuity of the Church of God from the Apostles' time, and would lead to an assertion that there exist in the Church particular

ministries for the shepherding of the flock and the building up of the whole body.)

The uniting Churches (stated if necessary) have sought to practise a continuity of such ministries by setting men apart with the authority of the Church for the ministry of Word and Sacrament. The united Church continues the orders of bishop, presbyter, and deacon as the Church of England previously received and continued them, and the respective functions of these three orders are sufficiently, though not exhaustively, set out in the services for ordaining ministers which follow.

Although the united Church receives the threefold orders that they 'may be continued, and reverently used and esteemed' (as was declared in the Preface to the 1550 and subsequent Anglican Ordinals), although it rules that none shall be ordained within its ministry save by a bishop and by the forms attached hereto, yet it receives also as presbyters in the Church of God those ministers of all the uniting Churches who make the requisite declaration in the presence of the bishop of their diocese, and are received by him with the requisite form.

THE REQUISITE DECLARATION
by Ministers of the Uniting Churches

I, A.B., having been ordained to the
                                    (ministry within the Church
                                    (priesthood within the Church
of God according to the rites of the
                                    (e.g. Methodist Church)
of God according to the rites of the
                                    Church of England)
                                                                do
now apply to you, bishop of —— in the united Church, for recognition and acceptance as a presbyter in the Church of God in the presbyterate of the united Church. I solemnly attest my acceptance of the confession of faith and constitution of this Church, and in particular of the threefold

structure of the ministry, and I promise that canonical obedience which is due from a presbyter to his bishop according to the constitution of this Church.

THE RECEPTION BY THE BISHOP

The Bishop shall stretch out his hands towards him and say:
I, A.B., bishop of —— in the united Church, do recognize and accept you as a presbyter in the Church of God, now to serve within the presbyterate of this diocese in the three-fold ministry of this Church. I now commit to you authority to exercise your ministry within this Church wherever you may be called and licensed. May God use your ministry to his great glory. (A blessing might then follow.)

EXPLANATORY NOTES ISSUED BY THE CHURCHES' UNITY COMMISSION

(1)

MUTUALLY ACCEPTABLE RITES (PROPOSITION 5)

1. *The Whole Rite of Christian Initiation*

Though we are simply describing the structure of these rites, it is nevertheless important to stress the importance of giving adequate instruction to the candidates about Christian faith and duty.

While there may properly be diversity of 'use', which should be fully allowed for, it is important that the essential elements of the whole process of Christian initiation be clearly understood.

The basic elements may be taken to be:

A) *A Scriptural passage* recalling the events of the life of our Lord to which the Church responds in its rites of initiation.

B) *An Act of profession of faith and commitment*

C) *Prayers at the Font or Baptistery.* After a rehearsal of the mighty acts of God, such prayer would appropriately include petition for God's continuing action in the power of the Spirit, that those baptized may be delivered from the dominion of sin into the freedom of the children of God; buried with Christ they may rise with him in newness of life; baptized into the one Body and so share in the one Spirit.

D) *The Act of Baptism.* This will be by water in the threefold name, and the *Laying on of hands* with the invocation of the Holy Spirit.

E) *Admission to Holy Communion*

2. *Varied Practice*

Since in the many Churches Christian initiation is not performed in its entirety at one time, we should note how the progression of the complete rite should be maintained.

A) *Baptism*
  a) *Scriptural Passages*
  b) *An Act of Confession and Commitment.* Where infant baptism is practised the parents should make confession of the Faith, and express commitment to the vocation of Christian parenthood – to the end that the child shall come to repent of sin, renounce evil, and turn to Christ.
  c) *Prayer at the Font or Baptistery*
  d) *The Act of Baptism* in water and in the threefold name.
B) *Confirmation*
  a) *Scriptural Passages*
  b) *An Act of Faith and Commitment*, which should involve the questions of the candidate about repentance and faith.
  c) *Invocation of the Holy Spirit and the Laying on of hands*
C) *Admission to the Holy Communion*

3. Where this basic pattern is followed, whether all its elements are administered at one time or at different times, the rites used are such as should be recognized by other Churches and, therefore, are mutually acceptable.

NB. It is assumed that within the Covenanting Churches those hitherto responsible for presiding at the act of confirmation will continue to do so.

The word 'confirmation' is here used to include the varied ways in which the Covenanting Churches entrust their members with the full privileges and responsibilities of membership.

February 1977

(2)

THE MEANING AND IMPLICATIONS
OF PROPOSITION 6
PREFACE

1. *The phrase 'episcopal, presbyteral and lay roles in ordination'*

For the purposes of this document it should be understood that in Proposition 6 'episcopal' refers not to a general exercise of oversight (episcope) but to the role of ministers specially set apart to a wide, crucial, and peculiarly responsible form of ministry distinguishable from the presbyteral ministry and from corporate and conciliar forms of oversight, though not exercised in separation from these; 'presbyteral' refers to the role of those who exercise a ministry of word and sacraments, whether as do the priests of the present episcopally ordered Churches or as do the ministers of those Churches which have a single form of the ministry of word and sacraments; 'lay' refers to the role of the laity both in the process leading to ordination (testing of candidature, training, call to a pastorate, decision to ordain) and in the act of ordination itself.

THE COMMON ORDINAL

2. In some traditions ordination is accompanied by more ceremonial than in others. It is not envisaged that there should be outward uniformity of practice, but that there should be agreed elements which should be found in all ordinations. The Common Ordinal should consist in a Preface setting forth the intention of the Service, and the essential elements of the rite of ordination which should include a service of the Word, the Presentation of the candidates, the Examination of them, and the Ordination Prayer. In many traditions, though not all, ordination takes place within the Eucharist. It should be open to Covenanting

Churches to add traditional elements regarded as explicating the meaning of the rite already performed.

MUTUAL ACCEPTANCE OF CHURCHES AND MINISTRIES

3. The fundamental point of reference is the ratification of the Covenant in a common act of worship which would include celebration of the mutual recognition of ministries. At this crucial point, the past, present and future of the partners involved are significantly affected.

a) In the context of mutual acceptance of one another as Churches in whose life Christ's word is proclaimed, his sacraments administered, and his *episcope* or oversight expressed, the ordained ministries of the Churches are recognized as true ministries of word and sacraments.

b) The ordained ministries (i.e. of the covenanting Churches) always universal in intention yet limited by their separation, seek and receive in God's sight full recognition from one another.

c) As solemnly committed to one another in mutual recognition and in the continued search for the visible unity that Christ intends for his people, the Churches enter a future in which each is mandated to foster, continue, and express in ministerial ordinations the new measure of fullness and universality.

4. The relationship into which Churches are invited to enter is one of deep and solemn commitment to each other and to the goal of visible unity, in the context of mutual recognition. The Churches thus become profoundly and visibly related yet remain distinguishable. Therefore two things are true. On the one hand, there would be no fundamental barrier to the full exercise of 'ministry' across denominational frontiers. On the other hand, the actual exercise of such ministry would properly remain subject in every case to the normal procedures whereby the denominations in question authorize it. No further ordination would be involved.

THE ROLE OF EPISCOPAL MINISTRY

5. The continuance, in respect of ministries, of the new measure of fullness and universality will imply particular attention being given to episcopal and presbyteral functions. In general, the Churches all prize and possess a presbyteral ministry of word and sacraments. Further, there is general recognition of and provision for expressions of *episcope* or oversight, and that in more than local fashion. Traditionally, however, *episcopacy* has been spoken of in connection with those (historically designated bishops) specially set apart to a wide, crucial, and peculiarly responsible form of ministry distinguishable from the presbyteral ministry and from corporate and conciliar forms of oversight, though not exercised in separation from these.

a) Such episcopal ministry is seen as a visible and significant expression of the unity and universality of the Church of God. Among its particular responsibilities in the past have been the safeguarding of the apostolic Faith and the provision of pastoral care for presbyters and people. The episcopal role at the heart of ordination has served to link new ministers to the Church in all places and all ages.

b) Within the diversity of the Christian tradition, the *functions* of episcope have been primarily located by some in individuals and by some in corporate bodies. Equally important, however, has been the widespread recognition that some such functions are best and most helpfully entrusted to individuals while others are more aptly and effectively committed to synods, councils, or assemblies. And either way it may be concluded that oversight, like all ministry, belongs firmly within the whole People of God and is never to be set in isolated fashion over against the Church it exists to serve.

c) Therefore to set down a distinguishable episcopal ministry as a mark of the Churches involved in the new commitment and the mutual recognition it carries with it is to speak of the setting apart of some to high responsibility, calling for considerable gifts of mind and spirit. To those who hitherto have not ordained to a distinct episcopal ministry, it is commended with conviction but without arrogance. Particular arguments from scripture or history have for long been variously evaluated, even within 'episcopal' Churches. In any event, it is episcopacy that is being commended, not one particular theory about it or a particular pattern of it. Rather is it the hope and expectation that the various Churches, learning from one another, may find patterns of episcopal ministry that will the more adequately serve the true ordering of the Body of Christ by the Gospel.

6. Thus far an account has been given of the role of episcopacy which could apply with equal force to various methods by which it may be accepted within the Covenanting Churches. At this point the Churches' Unity Commission wishes to set forth two alternative methods, each of which has attracted support from among its members, not (be it said) along clearly denominational lines. These alternatives, with their respective merits, are here presented to the participating Churches for fuller consideration.

METHOD A

7. Under this method Churches which at present lack a distinct episcopal ministry would be committed to its introduction and continuance within their life as an addition to the presbyteral ministry already prized and possessed. The way to this new departure would be opened for all participants by the common act of worship in which the Covenant is ratified and the mutual recognition of ministries is celebrated. The 'non-episcopal' Churches (as they are conventionally described) would proceed to the creation of an episcopal ministry which would be fully recognized as such by all the covenanting Churches. In these initial ordinations to the ranks of an emerging episcopate appro-

priate representatives of the covenanting Churches would associate themselves by word and action with such entry of new servants into the episcopal succession.

8. The introduction of such an episcopal ministry would lay upon a Church a double responsibility. On the one hand, there is required a faithful dealing with an inheritance. The episcopal ministry is to be welcomed as a visible and significant expression of the continuity, unity and universality of the Church of God through space and time. The central role of those who serve in the episcopal ministry in ordinations to the presbyteral ministry of word and sacraments is to be maintained. Yet there is equally required a faithful openness to whatever future the Lord of the Church intends. This implies a creative dealing with the inheritance which may hope to wrest from it more adequate patterns of episcopal ministry in function and in operation. Here as elsewhere the issue comes to the participating Churches in terms not so much of mutual accommodation as of common challenge.

9. That common challenge must surely be faced with both honesty and humility, with respect for the past and with openness to the future. The mutual recognition that is projected presses towards something more creative than a measure of interchange and movement across the frontiers of an unaltered co-existence. The 'non-episcopal' partners affirm the expressions of 'episcope' already existing within their own life, whatever name they bear, and question the 'episcopal' Churches as to the adequacy of their own episcopal practice, not least in the heavy concentration of episcopal functions within the office of bishop. The 'episcopal' partners affirm the office of bishop as a deeply-valued, long-enduring, unifying and sacramental focus of their own life and question the 'non-episcopal' Churches as to whether for the health and unity of the Church of God the focusing of some episcopal functions in a distinct office may not be Christian obedience in this hour.

10. Much depends on how such questions are posed and received. Even more, however, may depend upon a common willingness to question stereotypes and familiar models and do a new thing should loyalty to the Gospel and the imperatives of mission so demand. All the covenanting partners, searching their present Church life, may find episcopal functions being exercised in both corporate and individual ways.

11. It may then be clear that the mutual recognition of ministries, bound up as it is with historical controversy over episcopacy, is yet placed within the controlling context of the life and mission of the Churches today and to-morrow. The future is not necessarily served by taking over what lies to hand, by creating exact parallels to an existing episcopate, or by simply designating as bishops existing moderators, superintendents, or district chairmen. What may be required of all Churches is the creation of episcopal ministries that shall not only reflect their own ethos but also effectively serve the contemporary Church. Once more, diversity in unity may be the key.

METHOD B

12. The alternative proposal is that as from the accepted date all ordinations shall be acts in which all the covenanting Churches share in such a way that every future minister will be visibly commissioned by all the Churches to a ministry fully recognized throughout these Churches. The episcopal, presbyteral and lay roles will thus be expressed and opportunity be provided for sharing, within the process of growth towards visible unity, the gifts of ministry treasured within each of the Churches.

13. This proposal derives from the fact that the situation that will exist after covenanting will be very different from that which would follow an act of reunion. Separate Churches in covenant with each other would continue to

exist alongside each other, each with its own ministry and its own ordered life. The proposal that all these Churches should become episcopally ordered will not in itself extend the authority to minister within the other covenanting Churches. It would resolve the defects of our present ministries where these are seen as defects of order but would not so clearly remove the defects that spring from the disunity of the Church and which are more widely acknowledged.

14. This proposal may involve some alteration in the times and places at which ordinations are carried out but these areas of change, should they prove necessary, are regarded as matters of convenience and not of principle.

15. On this view the ministry thus ordained would point forward from the situation of Churches existing alongside one another, towards the discovery of a fuller unity. In acts of ordination it would be for the Churches to ensure that those representing them include those who carry the appropriate authority. The Common Ordinal would make provision for each to perform those acts through which his Church would normally confer ordination.

16. This proposal should not be regarded as concerned only with the act of ordination itself. Within the Covenant, it would lead to the development of ecumenical loyalties and responsibilities, though the discipline of each Covenanting Church would continue to be exercised towards its own members and ministers. It would lead naturally into ever-widening areas of decision-making in common and enable the still separate Churches increasingly to discover together their unity in Christ.

NOTE

17. In November 1976 the General Synod of the Church

of England expressed its desire that 'all the Covenanting Churches should become episcopally ordered in continuity with the historic episcopate'. The Churches' Unity Commission's response to this desire is given above. There remains, however, the question of the means whereby mutual recognition of ministries is to be achieved. The General Synod evidently wished to recommend to our attention the document GS 307 with its strong support for the approach of the *Groupe des Dombes*.

18. The Churches' Unity Commission has considered that document carefully, and warmly welcomes the *Groupe*'s recognition of the shared apostolicity of the Churches. It remains convinced that ratification of the Covenant is the decisive step in establishing mutual recognition of Churches and ministries. As already said, it believes that this ratification should be set within an act of worship, and it would be fitting that the mutual recognition should be marked by an outward and visible sign. The difficulties occasioned in the past by proposals which involve the laying on of hands (however intended) still seem hard to overcome. We therefore submit for further consideration the choice of the sign thought most appropriate, e.g. the giving of the Peace, the concelebration of Holy Communion, etc. All ordinations subsequent to the ratification of the Covenant should be according to the Common Ordinal.

19. Finally, it will be asked how, if Method A is adopted, the 'bishops' chosen by the Free Churches will be 'ordered in continuity with the historic episcopate'? We envisage the following stages, which could all be included in the one act of worship, if this were desired:
a) mutual acceptance of Churches and ministries through the ratification of the Covenant, as already described;
b) declaration that X, Y, Z have been chosen as bishops in the URC, Methodist Church, etc. . . .;
c) 'consecration' of all these by appropriate representatives of all the Covenanting Churches.

We see two advantages in this procedure: (i) the 'bishops' are chosen by the Churches themselves; (ii) all the Churches, as well as the Church of England, share in the 'consecration' of all of them. We think this provides authorization and continuity from all concerned.

THE QUESTION PUT TO THE CHURCHES BY MEANS OF PROPOSITION 6

20. The Commission asks the Churches whether they can proceed to mutual recognition of existing ministries as true ministries of word and sacraments in the Holy Catholic Church, on the basis of their present nature and exercise coupled with agreement that in future a common ordinal will be used which takes seriously the three roles, described in the first paragraph of this document.

21. The Commission has spelt out above both its general view of the relation between oversight (episcope) in general and the ministry of bishops in particular, and also two main ways in which an episcopal role in ordinations might be accepted during the period following the Covenant. This role is given special attention because of questions upon it addressed to the Commission in the interim responses from the Churches.

22. The Commission asks the Churches in their definitive responses to comment on its general view and to indicate whether either or only one (or neither) of these ways of receiving episcopal ministry is acceptable.

23. Thus a Church would have to answer 'No' to Proposition 6 if it felt obliged to require other conditions for mutual recognition of ministries, or if it were constrained to reject the future use of a Common Ordinal or to exclude one or more of the three roles. But a Church could answer 'Yes' to Proposition 6 on more than one understanding of what those roles might be.

24. The Commission cannot finalize proposals of its own until the definitive responses of the Churches make it clear how they are answering. There are four possibilities – a Church might answer 'No' to Proposition 6 for any of the above reasons. It might say 'Yes' to Methods A *and* B, as alternatives. Or it might say 'Yes' to A only or to B only.

January 1977

(3)

THE COMMON ORDINAL

INTRODUCTION

This Ordinal has been prepared for use in the Covenanting Churches. These are Churches in communion with one another but remaining distinct; they have judged their doctrinal agreement sufficient for a Covenant which includes mutual recognition of members and ministers; and they intend to learn from one another, to grow together and to come to a common understanding and exercise of ministry. Any advance towards visible unity in England that is to include the 'episcopal' Churches will involve the acceptance in some form by all the Covenanting Churches of the ministry of bishops and a basis must be found for harmony between the convictions concerning ministry in the Church held respectively by the Churches which at the time of the Covenant have bishops and those which do not.

If the Covenanting Churches agree to accept the ministry of bishops by Method A of the two described in the Commission's report of January 1977, then from the time of the Covenant a bishop of the Church whose candidates are to be ordained will preside at ordinations; it would be appropriate for him to be joined by bishops and ministers of other Churches, especially in the ordination of a bishop. Where ordinations of candidates from more than one

Church take place at the same time, the presidency of the service will be shared by the appropriate persons of the Churches concerned.

If the Covenanting Churches agree to accept the ministry of bishops by Method B, then from the time of the Covenant, the appropriate persons to preside from all the Covenanting Churches will take part in every ordination. The President will be the appropriate person of the Church whose candidates are to be ordained. A bishop will clearly be the appropriate participating representative of an episcopal Covenanting Church but will not be the presiding minister at ordinations for Churches which do not have bishops. Where ordinations of candidates from more than one Church take place at the same time, the presidency of the service will be shared by the appropriate persons of the Churches concerned.

Under both Methods ordination concerns more than the act of setting apart to the ministry. It implies a continuing relationship between those who ordain and those ordained. Within the Covenanting Churches each minister will be enabled increasingly to realize an ecumenical responsibility and loyalty towards the other Covenanting Churches and in particular to their leadership and oversight, both episcopal and conciliar. Each ministry will come to be exercised in a duel context in the developing common life and ministry of all the Covenanting Churches while under the discipline of one particular Church.

Under Method A where all the Covenanting Churches will have their own bishops, the continuing relationship between those who ordain and those who are ordained will be expressed by the way in which bishop and presbyters work together in each Church and in the Churches together.

Under Method B, common ordination initiates a relationship between those who ordain and those who are ordained which will immediately be set in a wider context than the particular Church in which ordination takes place; the continuation of this relationship in leadership and pastoral care will depend on the developing co-operation of the

Covenanting Churches. The fact that bishops participate in ordination will make explicit the acceptance by the Covenanting Churches of the positive values of episcopal ministry as described in the Commission's statement of January 1977 without changing the present ministerial order and discipline of those Churches.

Under either Method ministry will be exercised within a particular Church but will be capable of being extended to other Churches by their particular methods of authorization, without any question arising about ordination.

PREFACE TO THE ORDINAL
(This would *not* be read at Ordination Services)

MINISTRY IN THE CHURCH

God the Father sent his Son into the world to reconcile men and women to himself. He gathers those who believe in Jesus Christ's redeeming death and resurrection into one People by the gift of his Spirit. In the power of the Spirit Christ sends the Church into the world to preach the Gospel to the ends of the earth and to bring men and women in every age to knowledge of him.

Christ our Lord exercises his ministry in all members of his Body, the Church, for all are called and commissioned by their initiation to share in it. Though variously shared it is one ministry because it is Christ's. All ministries are gifts of the Holy Spirit for the building up of the Church to be the reconciled and reconciling community in the world.

THE ORDAINED MINISTRY

Particular responsibilities were assigned by Jesus in his lifetime, and in the Church from the beginning, to chosen disciples. The term 'apostle' is used in the New Testament for the foundational ministry of the Twelve, for Paul and others, and it comprises two main elements: a special relationship with the historical and risen Christ and a personal commission from him to the Church and the world. In the early Church particular responsibilities were variously exercised, but many of them came in time to be signified and conferred on specially chosen ministers by rites of ordination.

When the presbyterate emerged, it combined roles and ministries that had been distinct in the New Testament, notably: the particular discipleship of those called to commit themselves to the special service of the Gospel; the missionary proclamation of the Christian message; pastoral care of particular Christian communities; administration of baptism and presidency both at the Eucharist and at other central acts of Christian life. The president at the Eucharist began to be called 'priest' when the Eucharist came to be seen as having a sacramental relation to Christ's saving sacrifice.

Presbyters or bishops (the names seem at first to have been equivalent) succeeded the Apostles in their ministry of local pastoral responsibility and care. The growth and spread of the Church led to the development of the distinguishable ministries of presbyter and bishop. Responsibility for the wider Church, as originally exercised by the Apostles, came in time to be exercised by bishops, patriarchs and synods.

Various patterns of ordained ministry evolved through the years, but from this varied experience certain common principles are clear: these still hold good. The ordained ministry is both for the Church and for the world; its responsibility is to enable the whole Church to be fully the visible Body of Christ, glorifying the Father in and for the world. The ordained minister is a representative figure portraying to the Christian community Christ's Lordship and care of his people, and Christ's gathering of all his people into his own eternal worship of the Father.

Within the ordained ministry there is a sharing of responsibilities: the variety of roles and responsibilities exercised by presbyters can only be fulfilled by the presbyterate as a whole; whilst bishops have a particular responsibility to foster the unity and continuity of the Church through space and time in the apostolic faith, holiness and mission. Essential to the ordained ministry is its specific responsibility for oversight (episcope). Bishops and presbyters together exercise pastoral oversight of the Church and proclaim the Gospel by word and sacrament. This charge involves fidelity to the apostolic faith and mission, their embodiment in the contemporary Church, and their transmission to the Church of tomorrow.

At different times in the Church's life bishops and presbyters have been variously assisted by deacons; a variety of other ministries, some ordained and some not, have also played a part in the continuing life of the Church.

VOCATION AND ORDINATION

Ordination denotes entry into the apostolic and God-given ministry. Just as the original apostles did not choose themselves but were chosen and commissioned by Jesus, so those who are ordained are called by Christ in the Church and through the Church.

The President at ordination is one who by his office represents the unity between local congregations and their communion with the whole Church. (He is joined in the act of ordination by corresponding persons from other Covenanting Churches, so that collectively they represent the unity and continuity of the whole Church.)[1] Candidates who have been examined and accepted are ordained by the laying on of hands, with prayer that God will grant them the gift of the Holy Spirit for the ministry they are to exercise. The rite signifies and bestows on the ordinands the gift of sharing, within their calling, in the responsibilities of Christ's pastoral ministry; it shows that they are sealed and consecrated by the Spirit to manifest, within their calling, the holiness of the Father which he has revealed in

[1] The words in brackets apply particularly to Method B.

Christ; it commits them to a share in the prophetic ministry of Christ in the preaching of the Word; it declares the promise of divine grace as they share in the priestly ministry of Christ and of the whole Church and are conformed to the life of Christ, who took the form of a servant for our sake.

All ordinations have as their context the communion of the Churches and the historical continuity of their members with the Apostolic Church. In the ordination of a presbyter the presbyters present join with the President in praying for the gift of the Spirit and in the laying on of hands, thus signifying the shared nature of the commission entrusted to them. In the ordination of a bishop other bishops lay hands on him, as they request the gift of the Spirit for his ministry and receive him into their ministerial fellowship. This signifies that the new bishop and the people entrusted to his charge belong within the communion of Churches; and they stand in continuity with the Apostolic Church.

THE ORDINATION OF PRESBYTERS

Ordination shall take place in a service of Public Worship. In many traditions, ordination takes place within the Eucharist. It should be open to Covenanting Churches to add traditional elements regarded as explicating the meaning of the rite already performed.

The President will be assisted by presbyters and where customary lay people.[1] The Examination of the credentials of each ordinand will be handled by some appropriate procedure before the Service and only reported at the time of the Presentation.

---

[1] *For Method A* the President will be a bishop of the Church concerned.

For Method B the President will be the appropriate person of the Church concerned.

(See also the *Explanatory Note*.)

1) *A Service of the Word*

2) *The Presentation*

Following the sermon the person duly appointed shall present the ordinand(s) to the President.

We present these persons N.N. to be ordained as presbyters.

The President shall say to the congregation:

We intend, by God's grace, to ordain .... as presbyters. Those appointed by the Church to enquire about them and examine them have found them to be persons of sound learning and of Christian character and believe them to be duly called to serve God in this ministry. We ask you to declare your assent. Do you believe that these persons are by God's grace worthy to be ordained?

The people shall answer:

We believe that they are worthy. To God be the glory.

3) *The Examination*

The President shall address the candidates and say:

We are gathered here to ordain you as presbyters by prayer and the laying on of hands. A presbyter is one who shares in the priestly ministry of Christ and of the whole Church by preaching the Word, celebrating the sacraments, and leading the people in their mission to the world, exercising pastoral care, declaring the forgiveness of sins, taking a due place in administration and government, and being conformed to the life of Christ who took the form of a servant for our sake.

As presbyter, it will be your task to proclaim the Gospel by your words and in your life. You are to love, serve and pray for all the people among whom you work, caring alike for young and old, strong and weak, rich and poor. Understand the meaning of what you do – practise what you profess – always remember that you are to serve rather than be served, to look after the concerns of Christ and not your own.

Therefore, that we may know that you confess the Christian Faith and are resolved to fulfil the ministry to which you have been called,

I ask you:

Do you believe in One God, Father, Son and Holy Spirit?

I do.

Do you believe that the Scriptures of the Old and New Testaments, interpreted under the guidance of the Holy Spirit, provide the supreme standard for the faith and life of all God's people?

I do.

Do you believe in your heart that you are truly called of God into this sacred ministry, with all its obligations and opportunities for the service of God and man?

I do.

Do you promise to fulfil the duties of your calling with all fidelity, to lead the people committed to your charge in worship, to preach the Word and administer the Sacraments, to exercise pastoral care and oversight, to minister God's forgiveness of sins, and to give leadership to the Church in its mission to the world?

I do.

Will you strive to live a holy life, being diligent in prayer, and always maintaining the truths of the Gospel, whatever troubles or persecution may arise?

I will.

Will you be loyal to the Church in which you are to minister, accepting its order and discipline, to the end that it may more and more serve the will of God for this world?

I will.

Will you seek the peace and unity of all Christ's people according to his will?

I will.

And all these things do you believe and promise as the Lord Jesus Christ shall give you grace and strength to fulfil the same?

By the help of God, I do.

May God who has given you the will to do all these things, grant you also grace to perform them, that he may accomplish the work which he has begun in you, through Jesus Christ our Lord.

Faithful is he who calls you, and he will not fail you.

Amen

4) *Ordination*

After a hymn invoking the Holy Spirit, the ordinands kneel, and the President shall say:

Let us pray:

Eternal God, Creator and Preserver, we praise you for your infinite love and goodness towards us and all mankind. We praise you that you chose a people for your own out of our sinful humanity to become a royal priesthood and a holy nation, offering to you love and acceptable worship. We praise you that in the fulness of time you gave your only Son Jesus Christ to become our Saviour and the author of everlasting life.

We praise you that by his death and resurrection he has overcome death, and that, having ascended into heaven, he has poured forth his gifts abundantly upon your people, making some apostles, some prophets, some evangelists, some pastors and teachers, for the building up of his body the Church and for the fulfilling of your purpose in the world. And now we give you thanks that you have called these your servants to share this ministry entrusted to your Church.

(*For Method A*
Here the Bishop says the ensuing prayer as in company with others appointed he lays his hands on the head of each person to be ordained; or he says the prayer once over all the candidates and then lays his hands in silence on each of them, his assistants doing likewise.)

(*For Method B*
Here the President together with the representatives of the other Covenanting Churches says the ensuing prayer as they lay their hands on the head of each person to be ordained; or they may say the prayer once over all the candidates and then lay their hands in silence on each of them. The others from the Church concerned who are assisting the President shall then lay their hands in silence on each candidate.)

> Therefore, O Father, we pray, send your Holy Spirit upon your servant, N......... whom we in your name and in obedience to your will, do now ordain presbyter in your Church, with authority to minister your Word and Sacraments, and to shepherd your flock.

(Each time this petition is made, the people shall answer, Amen.)

Then the President shall continue:

> Give abundantly, O God, to these your servants the grace they need to serve you in this ministry. Make them faithful pastors, patient teachers, and wise counsellors. Endue them with clear insight, honest thought, and forthrightness of speech to make known the good news of your salvation. Enable them in all things to fulfil their ministry faithfully and to offer with all your people spiritual sacrifices acceptable to you, through Jesus Christ our Lord.

Amen

The President or one of his assistants may deliver the Holy Scripture into the hands of each presbyter, saying: Take the Holy Scriptures, a token of the authority you have been given to preach the Word of God and to celebrate the Sacraments.

The President and those assisting him may give the right hand of fellowship to the newly-ordained presbyters.

May 1977

(4)

COMMENT ON PROPOSITION 7

From the outset the Commission has always maintained that visible unity does not require visible uniformity. Nor in the Ten Propositions are they proposing a particular scheme of structural unity. In the immediate post-covenant period, the covenanting Churches will in fact continue to function with their present institutional structures little altered save for the significant acceptance of episcopacy. Mutual recognition does not of itself convey multiple membership, nor does it release individuals from the authority and discipline of that particular communion to which they have been admitted as members.

Consciences are formed by the *experience* of community worship and of faith, mediating the truth given by God into the realities of the present. In the common life of believers within the fellowship of the covenanting Churches it will be discovered that there is a greater consensus on matters of faith and doctrine than is generally believed. To quote from the Roman Catholic provisional response: 'Our present growth in unity argues that there is a deeper consensus in this area than our present divisions seem to indicate.'

The exercise of rights of conscience may be expected to cause discomfort or to raise questions in the minds of those who see things in a different light. This calls for humility on the one side, and toleration on the other. Only so can those who differ dwell together in unity.

There are numerous issues which may emerge as matters

of individual conscience: such as the acceptability of women's ministry; questions of marriage discipline; the admissibility of 're-baptism'; teaching on contraception. These can only be resolved for an individual by appeal to the acknowledged authorities of his denomination. Although freedom of conscience is allowed to individuals, the Covenanting Churches will not be at liberty to take actions which conflict with the Covenant into which they have entered.

At present members of each denomination can expect their own Church carefully to consider their case when they claim rights of conscience. The fact of covenanting should not put them in a less advantageous position than they were before.

May 1977